Pat the ^Great Cat

A JAGUAR'S JOURNEY

Children of the Americas

tell a true story of a very

noble jaguar

SHARP
Literacy, Inc.
Student Historical Art Resource Program

This book was produced by SHARP Literacy, Inc.
using the works submitted by students.

PAT THE CAT: FACT OR FICTION?

Pat the Cat is a very real jaguar from the beautiful country of Belize, Central America. His story is true! Now, because jaguars try to stay far away from people, no one came to know about Pat until his first unfortunate contact with humans. Because of this, the story of his early life is based upon what we know about how jaguars live in the wild. Certainly he had a mother, and very likely at least one sister (or brother). Pat's life before people moved into his territory is based upon what is likely to have happened to him. But each and every fact in the rest of the story really happened. This type of story is called narrative non-fiction.

The story you are about to read is part of a special literacy program that brought together many of Pat's friends—the children of Belize, Central America, and the children of Milwaukee, Wisconsin, USA—to write a book about this noble cat. First, the children listened to the story of Pat the Cat in a special presentation of "Pat the Cat: The Jaguar Diaries." They were excited! The children spent many hours researching and writing about Pat and about the world of the jaguar. They also drew pictures, and wrote songs, poems, and letters. Their work was combined and edited to become the book you are about to read. Lots of people came together to write Pat's story! The beautiful narrative was woven together by Bethany Ganz O'Day from a story by Nancy Kennedy.

Children from all over have joined together to continue writing about Pat, and about the wild world of the jaguar. We hope that you, too, will count yourself as a friend of the elusive jaguar, the last great cat of the Americas. Pat lost his freedom in the beautiful rainforest of Belize, but if you are reading this book, his loss of freedom will not be in vain. For that, Pat, and all of his friends, thank you.

SHARP Literacy, Inc. is a nonprofit 501(c)(3) educational organization.

Published by SHARP Literacy, Inc., 750 North Lincoln Memorial Drive, Suite 311
Milwaukee, Wisconsin 53202-4018
USA
www.sharpliteracy.org

Graphic Designer: Dan Saal
Illustrator: Francisco X. Mora
Photographer of Illustrations: Sonja Thomsen
Spanish Translation: Alessandra Luiselli
Printer: Quad/Graphics Commercial and Specialty

First Edition
9 8 7 6 5 4 3 2 1

Printed in the United States of America

Library of Congress Control Number: 2011930996

ISBN 978-0-983-6222-1-5 Hardcover

ISBN 978-0-983-6222-0-8 Softcover

CONTENTS

8   Pat the ^(Great) Cat: A Jaguar's Journey

ACKNOWLEDGMENTS

The joyful task of producing the beautiful book you hold in your hands is the result of many dedicated and talented people who deserve most grateful thanks.

This book would not have happened without Marlene Doerr and her SHARP Literacy team, dedicated professionals who instill a love of reading and writing, enriched through the visual arts, to nearly six thousand children each and every year. Along with the SHARP staff, special presentation teams in Milwaukee and Belize brought Pat's story to life for the children, and witnessed the classroom joy: Leann Beehler, Celso Poot, Jamal Andrewin, and Barbara Thummalapally. Our work was made richer by Dr. Bruce Beehler, Deputy Director of the Milwaukee County Zoo; our science partners at Panthera, Dr. Howard Quigley, Molly Parrish, and Andrea Heydlauff (whose award-winning film "My Pantanal" delighted the children); and our curriculum team at SUNY Cortland, headed by Dr. Tom Pasquarello. We would not have been able to connect the children of our two countries without the support and encouragement of the Belize Ministry of Education, through the guiding hand of Ms. Rose Bradley. The book was lovingly created through the mystical and moving illustrations of Francisco X. Mora, the graphic design of Dan Saal, and the beautiful writing of Bethany Ganz O'Day. Special thanks to Sara Liebert for her leadership, Dr. Patricia Ellis for her innovative ideas, Dr. Alessandra Luiselli for her beautiful translation, and to the great team at Quad/Graphics. Those who have cared for Pat will never be forgotten: Sharon Matola, Humberto Wohlers, Bladimir Miranda, Neil Dretzka, Valerie Werner, Chris John, and Celi Jeske. Special thanks also to filmmakers Richard Foster and Carol Farneti Foster, who used their incredible footage of the wildlife that lived along the banks of the Raspaculo River, to bring the magic of Belize into the classrooms of Milwaukee where the children could truly experience the world of the jaguar. Heartfelt thanks to Bill and Geralyn Cannon, Madonna and Jay Williams, Peggy Schuemann, Jonathan Adelman, and Jason Mraz. Finally, to the love of my life and my inspiration, who started it all with his love of big cats, my husband, John.

This book is dedicated to the beautiful and talented children of Milwaukee and Belize who took Pat the Cat into their hearts and brought his story to the world, and to an angel named Julian, a little boy from Belize who loved jaguars.

Nancy M. Kennedy | September 2011

Amazing and talented children in the following schools participated in this special project:

Blessed Sacrament Elementary School, Milwaukee

Buena Vista Government School, Belize

The Business and Economics Academy of Milwaukee

Eden Seventh Day Adventist Primary School, Belize

Escuela Vieau School, Milwaukee

Forest Home Avenue Elementary School, Milwaukee

Greenfield Bilingual Elementary School, Milwaukee

Hartford University School for Urban Exploration, Milwaukee

Hattieville Government School, Belize

Institute of Technology and Academics, Milwaukee

Albert E. Kagel School, Milwaukee

Richard Kluge Elementary School, Milwaukee

Lloyd Street Global Education School, Milwaukee

Longfellow Elementary School, Milwaukee

Louisiana Government School, Belize

Parklawn Christian Leadership Academy, Milwaukee

Rogers Street Academy, Milwaukee

St. Agnes Anglican Primary School, Belize

St. Jude Roman Catholic School, Belize

St. Martini Lutheran School, Milwaukee

Trowbridge School of Discovery and Technology, Milwaukee

Victory School for the Gifted and Talented, Milwaukee

LETTER FROM EXECUTIVE DIRECTOR

Dear Students,

When I started SHARP Literacy, I did so with the desire to help open a creative world of reading and learning for all our students. I could not have imagined all the wonderful people I would meet and all the interesting things I would learn in the process. I always try to keep an open mind and a positive attitude. You just never know what you can learn from each person and experience you encounter every single day.

We hope you will find Pat's story inspiring. You certainly will learn about jaguars, but you will also learn about people. No matter where they live, no matter what language is spoken, whether the people are wealthy or poor, we all need to take care of one another and our environment.

Every single day throughout your life I hope you will look around to see where you can help. Each small act of kindness will have a positive result. You don't have to be an adult to make changes in the world. Something as simple as a smile can make a big difference to someone who's having a hard day. Picking up trash in your neighborhood, being kind to animals, or helping an older person with tasks they have difficulty doing, are all great ways to make a difference. Keep your eyes open and you will be amazed how you too can help. Each of us can make a difference and help make our world a better place. Pat's caretakers helped make a difference for him, and in turn, Pat is teaching people about many things, especially about jaguars. Each little positive action taken by individuals can build to make big changes in your neighborhood, and in our world! Please enjoy reading this beautiful book.

Hugs to all of you.

Marlene M. Doerr

Marlene M. Doerr
Executive Director | SHARP Literacy, Inc.

Special thanks to our donors

John and Nancy Kennedy

Johnson Controls Foundation

Rockwell Automation

Harley-Davidson Foundation

Pentair Foundation

Vinai and Barbara Thummalapally

Puelicher Foundation

Zoological Society of Milwaukee

FOREWORD

Many years ago, hearing the word Balam would have been enough to make you tremble and kneel immediately; it meant you were in the presence of the most powerful creature of Mayan Mythology: Balam.

Balam was the name given by the Mayas to the mighty jaguar. In his role as the mightiest of the Celestial Messengers, Balam also signified The Lord of the Jungle, The Guardian of the Earth, and The One Who Holds the Darkness.

Balam was the mighty being who announced the arrival of all new things. Balam was the entity who each night fought a battle against the day, thus maintaining the balance of the Universe. Temples, built in honor of Balam, contained "estelas" depicting Mayan kings sitting next to a Jaguar, symbolizing their common celestial bloodline.

The Spirit of the Jaguar was also recognized and revered among other ancient civilizations of America. Aztec warriors proudly carried the Ocelotl (Jaguar) surname, synonymous with valor and courage. The Olmecs considered facial features to be of beauty if they resembled those of the Jaguar.

This book invites you to follow the journey of one such magnificent creature as seen through the eyes of Pat the *Royal* Cat. We hope this story is entertaining, but we also hope it causes you to consider the responsibility we have for nature's creatures.

Think of how it may affect our future if we don't accept that responsibility, and how important it is that we help maintain balance as we shape the habitat of others, those who once were known as the Celestial Messengers.

Francisco X. Mora

INTRODUCTION

"There is a cat in this world that really puts a spark in my eye. His name is Pat." I wish that you could have seen the excitement in the eyes of the children of Milwaukee and of Belize, whose work is represented here, when they first heard the story of our very special jaguar, Pat the Cat. In these difficult times, Pat's journey resonated strongly in their own lives: challenge, loss, fear, change, love, hope, opportunity, acceptance, meaning, joy. Guided by some of the most dedicated teachers in the world, the children responded with an avalanche of material. Some of the children created their own blog. Others asked that a website be created so that they could reach out in real time to children and teachers the world over. And so patthegreatcat.com was born, to bring more of their work to the world than could be contained in the pages that follow.

"One astonishing day in Belize, a cat was born." Wanting to make a difference, our children have become authors and advocates, artists and motivators. Children and teachers in Colorado, Pennsylvania, and Florida heard about their work and are joining in, all because of the real-life story of a jaguar named Pat, and the love of learning ignited by real stories and experiences that excite them and expand their world.

"Pat lived in Belize. Anyone would love to live there. I think that Pat loved his home." It matters not that the children who participated in the project live in different villages, cities, states, or countries. Together, as children of the Americas, they have taken on the challenge of teaching us about the jaguar, our great *American* cat. In the process, we all discover that the world is really a much smaller place than we imagined.

"It is our turn to protect the jaguar—the last great cat of the Americas." The children have worked very hard to make an impact through their research, their writing, and their interest in and compassion for one another and for our natural world. They have inspired me, as I hope they will inspire you. Join us in this adventure, and bring along a child you love.

Nancy M. Kennedy

"He is a **noble** jaguar."

Pat the ^Great Cat

A JAGUAR'S JOURNEY

El Gran Gato Pat: Viajes de un Jaguar

Soy un jaguar. Crecí en la hermosa selva tropical de Belice, en Centroamérica, acechando presas y durmiendo en cuevas. Cuando me rompí la pata, no podía cazar más, estuve a punto de morir de hambre. Alguien casi me mató entonces, pero, gracias a algunos amigos, encontré una nueva vida. Esta es mi historia.

I am a jaguar.
I grew up in the beautiful rainforest of Belize in Central America, stalking prey and sleeping in caves. When I broke my leg, I couldn't hunt any more. I nearly starved to death. Then someone almost killed me, but thanks to some friends, I found a new life.

This is my story.

Jaguars are special because they belong to us. The jaguar is the great American cat!

Los jaguares son especiales porque son nuestros, nos pertenecen. El jaguar es el gran gato de América.

NORTH AMERICA
(Norteamérica)

CENTRAL AMERICA
(Centroamérica)

SOUTH AMERICA
(Sudamérica)

Jaguars are the only great cats of the Americas. The Americas include North, Central, and South America.

Únicamente los jaguares son los grandes gatos de las Américas. Las Américas incluyen: Norte, Centro y Sudamérica.

CHAPTER 1

Pat the Cub

I was just a cub, dreaming of flying through the dark sky, high above the rainforest of Belize. I was soaring like a bird, alone. Where was my mother? Where was my sister? I felt I had to be flying for a reason. What was it? Then I awoke to the smell of the earth that lined the snug den I shared with my family.

My mother had dug our den in the dark soil between the roots of a great kapok tree. My sister was sleeping next to me. I knew my mother was out hunting. My stomach growled at the thought of the fresh meat she would bring to us. She might bring a turtle or maybe an anteater. I yawned. My sister snored. I rolled against her warm fur.

When we were younger, my sister and I never left the safety of the den. Our mother gave us her milk and left us alone only to hunt for her own food.

El cachorro Pat

Yo sólo era un cachorro, soñando con volar a través del cielo oscuro, por lo alto de la selva tropical de Belice. Yo planeaba en las alturas, solo como un pájaro. ¿Dónde estaba mi madre? ¿Dónde estaba mi hermana? Sentía que tenía que estar volando por una razón. ¿Cuál era? Me desperté entonces con el olor de la tierra que se alineaba en la acogedora guarida que compartía con mi familia.

Mi madre había cavado nuestra guarida, en la tierra, entre las raíces de una gran ceiba. Mi hermana dormía junto a mí. Yo sabía que mi madre estaba afuera, cazando. Ante la idea de la carne fresca que nos traería, mi estómago gruñó. Ella podría traernos una tortuga o, tal vez, un oso hormiguero. Bostecé. Mi hermana roncó. Me di la vuelta, quedando muy cerca de su tibio pelaje.

Cuando mi hermana y yo éramos pequeños nunca nos apartábamos de la seguridad de nuestra guarida. Mi madre nos amamantaba y únicamente nos dejaba solos para salir a cazar su propia comida.

Baby jaguars are called cubs, just like baby bears and lions. Mother jaguars usually have one or two cubs, but sometimes they have three.

A las crías de los jaguares se les llama cachorros, igual que a las crías de osos y leones. Las madres jaguares usualmente tienen uno o dos cachorros, pero algunas veces tienen tres.

In Belize, the kapok tree is called the ceiba (say-buh) tree.

En Belice al arbol kapok se le llama ceiba.

Jaguar cubs are blind until they are about two weeks old.

Las crías del jaguar son ciegas hasta que tienen aproximadamente dos semanas de edad.

The word jaguar comes from the word, *yaguara.* It means "beast that kills its prey in a single jump."

La palabra jaguar viene del vocablo yaguara, que significa "bestia que mata sus presas con un solo salto."

Before long, he was a curious and frisky cub!

En poco tiempo era un curioso y juguetón cachorro.

The scientific name for jaguar is *panthera onca.*

El nombre científico para el jaguar es *Panthera Onca.*

Now we were older and bigger. We didn't need milk anymore. Our mother had taught us to hunt small prey, like mice and young iguanas. Why should I wait to eat until she returned when I could hunt for my own food?

I left my sleeping sister and padded silently out of the den. I sniffed the air, hoping to catch the scent of something to eat, but there was nothing. I heard the rush of the nearby waterfall and thought of the turtles swimming in the pool below the falls. Turtle sounded good. I'd never ventured that far alone before, but my hunger called to me. Besides, I reminded myself, I was a jaguar, a hunter.

I moved swiftly through the forest toward the water. I could surely capture my own meal before my mother returned from her long hunt. Sometimes she was gone for hours, roaming over ten miles (16 kilometers) in search of the tasty peccary or the long-tailed spider monkey.

Luego crecimos y nos volvimos más grandes y fuertes. Ya no necesitábamos tomar leche. Nuestra madre nos había enseñado a cazar presas pequeñas, como ratones e iguanas. Entonces ¿por qué debía esperar a comer hasta que ella regresara si yo podía cazar mi propia comida?

Dejé a mi hermana dormida y, en silencio, salí de la guarida. Olfateé el aire, esperando percibir el olor de algo para comer, pero no detecté nada. Oí el sonido de una cascada cercana y pensé en las tortugas nadando bajo el torrente de agua. Una tortuga me sabría bien. Nunca antes me había aventurado a salir tan lejos, pero el hambre me dominaba. Además recordé que yo era un jaguar, un cazador.

Me moví ágilmente a través de la selva tropical, hacia la cascada. Seguramente podría apresar mi comida antes que mi madre regresara de su larga cacería. A veces ella se iba por horas, recorriendo más de diez millas (16 kilómetros) buscando el sabroso pecarí o el mono araña de larga cola.

Soon I arrived at the shallow pool at the base of the waterfall. I smelled something strange. The hair on the back of my neck prickled, but what was there to fear? I'd been to the pool many times with my mother for swimming lessons. I heard a soft splash and saw a small turtle swimming near the edge of the water.

I crouched low the way my mother had shown me. I carefully lifted one paw and took a step—slowly, slowly. The turtle stopped. I stopped. Staring, I could almost taste the juicy meat. I took another slow step and then another until I was close enough to pounce. I tensed my muscles for the final leap, but something was wrong. There was that strange smell again–much stronger now. My whiskers twitched. I took my eyes from the turtle and looked down at my feet. Too late! A poisonous coral snake was moving in to bite me.

Llegué rápido al estanque de agua poco profunda en la base de la cascada. Olí algo extraño. El pelaje de mi cuello se erizó, tenía miedo, pero ¿qué era lo que debería temer? Había estado en el estanque varias veces con mi madre, aprendiendo a nadar. Oí un tenue ruido y vi una tortuguita nadando cerca de la orilla.

Me encogí de la manera que me había enseñado mi madre. Cuidadosamente levanté una pata y di un primer paso, despacio, muy despacio. La tortuga se detuvo. Yo también me detuve. Mirándola fijamente casi podía casi saborear su jugosa carne. Di otro lento paso y después otro, hasta que estuve lo suficientemente cerca para atacar. Tensé todos mis músculos para el salto final, pero algo andaba mal. Era ese extraño olor de nuevo, mucho más fuerte ahora. Mis bigotes se contrajeron. Desvié la vista de la tortuga y miré hacia mis patas. ¡Demasiado tarde! Debajo de mí se arrastraba una venenosa serpiente coral dispuesta a morderme.

In the wild, cubs lead a dangerous life. They must fend for themselves before leading independent lives.

En la naturaleza los cachorros tienen una vida peligrosa. Deben aprender a valerse por sí mismos antes de llevar una vida independiente.

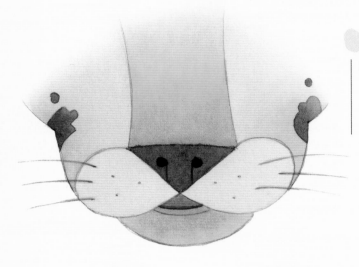

All cats have whiskers that help them sense things around them.

Todos los gatos tienen bigotes que los ayudan a percibir cosas a su alrededor.

De repente escuché un rugido sordo, y vi el brillo de los dientes de mi madre mordiendo la cabeza de la serpiente. Ella sacudió fuertemente a la serpiente y la arrojó a un lado. Luego corrió hacia mí y me lamió la cara y el cuello.

La seguí de regreso a la guarida donde mi hermana ya estaba comiendo el gran oso hormiguero mi madre había traído para la comida.

Pasaría mucho tiempo antes de que yo volviera a salir a cazar solo.

Suddenly **I heard a rumbling roar,** and I saw the flash of my mother's teeth bite down on the snake's head. She shook the snake and threw it aside. Then she rushed to me and licked my face and neck.

I followed her back to the den where my sister was already eating the fat anteater my mother had brought for dinner.

It would be a long time before I went out again to hunt on my own.

Pat is a cat. He belongs to the feline family, but he isn't your typical house cat. He is a wild animal.

Pat es un gran gato. Pertenece a la familia de los felinos, pero no es el típico gato que vive en una casa. Es un animal salvaje.

Jaguars are really neat animals, very pretty, but they do not make good pets!

Los jaguares son animales realmente muy bonitos pero ino son buenas mascotas!

CHAPTER 2

Pat the Hunter

As time passed, I grew. My fuzzy, gray, cub fur smoothed to a sleek golden yellow coat, dotted with black rosette spots. My blue eyes changed to a fiery yellow. My sister grew too. She was a beautiful black jaguar. Sometimes jaguars are born black and stay black. Their dark fur is dotted with even darker rosettes.

Almost fully grown now, I was nearly five feet long, not including my tail. I was taller than my sister, taller even than my mother, and I weighed more than 100 pounds (45 kilograms). My muscles had become strong. I had learned my mother's lessons well and no longer feared any animal in the forest. I was an apex predator. I was at the top of the food chain.

No other animal in the rainforest would dare to hunt me.

El cazador Pat

Con el pasar del tiempo, crecí. El tono gris de mi pelaje de cachorro cambió y se convirtió en una brillosa y elegante capa de tonos amarillos y dorados cubierta de negras rosetas. Mis ojos azules cambiaron a un amarillo intenso. Mi hermana también creció. Ella se convirtió en un hermoso jaguar negro. Algunas veces los jaguares nacen negros y así permanecen siempre. Su piel oscura está cubierta de rosetas aun más oscuras.

Ahora, ya crecido casi totalmente, yo medía casi cinco pies de largo, sin incluir la cola; era más alto que mi hermana e incluso más alto que mi madre, pesaba más de 100 libras (45 kilogramos). Mis músculos se hicieron fuertes. Yo había aprendido muy bien las lecciones que me había dado mi madre y no le temía a ningún animal en la selva tropical. Yo estaba en la cima como depredador. Ocupaba el lugar más alto en la cadena alimentaria animal.

Ningún otro animal de la selva tropical se atrevería a cazarme.

The color and markings of the jaguar are its own glory. Every coat is individual!

El color y las rosetas del jaguar son el orgullo de este animal. Cada piel es única.

Jaguars look a lot like leopards, but if you look carefully, you can see the difference.

Los jaguares se parecen mucho a los leopardos, pero si observas detenidamente podrás notar la diferencia.

Rosettes

The spots on a jaguar are called rosettes because they look like roses. Jaguars have one or two black dots in the middle of their rosettes.

Rosetas

Las manchas en la piel de los jaguares se llaman rosetas porque parecen rosas. En el centro de sus rosetas los jaguares tienen uno o dos puntos negros.

Leopards and jaguars both have dark yellow or orange coats covered with rosettes. Leopards do not have spots in the middle of their rosettes, but jaguars do. Jaguars have thicker bodies and shorter tails than leopards.

Los leopardos y los jaguares tienen ambos piel amarilla oscura o anaranjada, cubierta de rosetas. Los jaguares tienen manchas en el centro de sus rosetas; los leopardos no. Los jaguares son más corpulentos y sus colas son más cortas que los leopardos.

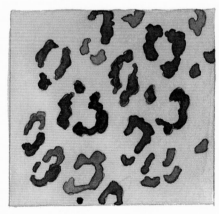

Leopard (Leopardo)

Jaguar (Jaguar)

Tiger (Tigre)

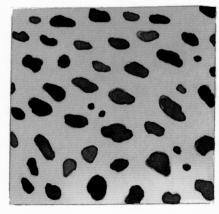

Cheetah (Guepardo)

Jaguars hunt mostly at dawn and dusk. Their excellent senses of smell, sight, and hearing help them find their prey.

Los jaguares cazan casi siempre al amanecer o al anochecer. Sus excelentes sentidos del olfato, vista y oído les ayudan a encontrar sus presas.

Jaguars are great hunters.

Los jaguares son grandes cazadores.

A jaguar doesn't make noise when he is hunting his prey.

El jaguar no hace ruido cuando está cazando a su presa.

Now you see it, now you don't.
The undercover hunter!

Ahora lo ves, ahora no.
Es el cazador encubierto.

When I was bigger, we moved to a cool, dry cave. I slept there most days during the wet season to the sound of rain splashing in the forest. At night I would often leave my mother and sister to hunt alone.

One night I stayed out so late that it was almost dawn. The moon was still shining in the sky, casting patterns of light and shadow on the forest floor. My spotted coat blended in with the moonlight and shadows. My camouflage made me **almost invisible** as I moved silently through the forest.

Cuando crecí más, nos mudamos a una cueva fresca y seca. Yo dormía ahí durante las temporadas de lluvias, con el sonido de la lluvia salpicando la selva. Con bastante frecuencia dejaba a mi madre y a mi hermana y me iba a cazar solo.

Una noche salí y me quedé fuera casi hasta que estaba a punto de amanecer. La luna todavía brillaba en el cielo, proyectando diseños de luz y sombra en el suelo de la selva. Mi pelaje se confundía con la luz de la luna y las sombras. Mientras me movía en silencio por la selva, mi camuflaje me volvía casi invisible.

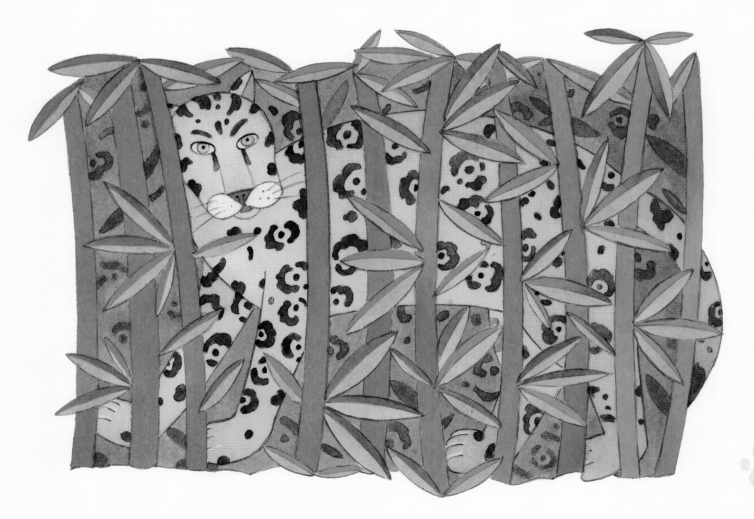

All good hunters are sneaks,
and cats are the sneakiest!

Todos los cazadores son furtivos, los
grandes gatos son los más cautelosos.

Peccary

A peccary is a pig-like animal with small legs,
thick neck, short fur, and a snout.

Pecarí

El pecarí se parece al cerdo, tiene patas cortas,
cuello grueso, pelaje muy corto y hocico.

Peccaries travel in herds, numbering
up to fifty members.

Los pecaríes viajan en manadas, pueden llegar
a ser hasta cincuenta el número de miembros
de una manada.

There was the scent of fresh rain. The sound of howler monkeys filled the air. I smelled small prey, birds, and an armadillo nearby. Fainter and more distant was the enticing scent of white-lipped peccary. I followed the scent through the forest, slowing my pace and moving carefully as the scent grew stronger. I could hear the peccaries rooting with their snouts for fallen fruit.

I crouched low in the thick ferns, careful to stay upwind so the peccaries could not smell me. I watched silently until one of the fat animals wandered away from the others. I climbed up a mahogany tree and out onto a large limb until I was directly above the lone peccary. The thick branch bent with my weight, but it did not break.

Había un olor a lluvia fresca. El sonido de los monos aulladores llenaba el aire. Percibí el cercano olor de pequeñas presas, pájaros y un armadillo. Un poco más tenue y lejano percibí el seductor olor del pecarí de blancos labios. Seguí ese olor a través de la selva, reduciendo mi paso y moviéndome con sumo cuidado cuando el olor se volvía más fuerte. Podía escuchar a los pecaríes hurgando las frutas caídas con sus hocicos.

Me escondí entre los espesos helechos, cuidando de mantenerme contrario al viento para que los pecaríes no pudieran olerme. En silencio observé hasta que uno de los animales más grandes se alejó de los demás. Me trepé entonces a un árbol de caoba, permanecí oculto sobre una gran rama que se extendía hasta quedar directamente arriba del solitario pecarí. La rama se dobló con mi peso, pero no se rompió

The mahogany is the national tree of Belize. Its reddish wood is used for furniture, bowls, and decorative carvings.

La caoba es el árbol nacional de Belice. Su madera rojiza se usa para la fabricación de muebles, vasijas y artesanías.

Then, with one powerful jump,

I landed on the peccary's back and sank my teeth into its head, killing it instantly. Snapping their jaws and barking, the other peccaries rushed toward me. I leapt quickly back to the mahogany branches, away from the peccaries' trampling feet. I waited until they ran off into the forest, clicking their teeth in alarm. I climbed out of the tree and dragged my heavy kill under some bushes to keep it safe.

I would return later with my mother and sister to feast.

Entonces, con un poderoso salto, caí en la espalda del pecarí, le hundí mis dientes en la cabeza, matándolo instantáneamente. Los otros pecaríes se abalanzaron hacia mí, crujiendo sus mandíbulas y ladrando. Rápidamente me trepé de un salto al árbol de caoba, lejos del ruidoso estrépito de los pecaríes. Esperé hasta que corriendo huyeron hacia más adentro de la selva, chocando sus dientes como forma de alarma. Bajé del árbol y arrastré a mi pesada presa muerta hasta dejarla escondida y segura entre los arbustos.

Regresaría más tarde al festín de comerla, con mi madre y hermana.

Jaguars are not fast runners. They have strong shoulders and front legs. Their back legs are long, making it easy for them to jump.

Los jaguares no son corredores muy rápidos. Tienen hombros y patas delanteras fuertes. Sus patas traseras son largas, esto hace que para ellos sea muy fácil dar grandes saltos.

Jaguars are carnivores and, gee, do they love their meat!

Los jaguares son carnívoros y ¡vaya que aman su carne!.

CHAPTER 3

Pat's Beautiful Home

In the dry season, when it was cooler, I liked to sun myself on a rock above the waterfall. Sometimes I slept, but often I just rested in the beauty of the rain forest. One day several keel-billed toucans were hopping along the branches of a nearby tree croaking "rrrrk! rrrrk!" Their yellow-feathered chests and rainbow beaks filled the tree with color. Passion fruit vines were wrapped around the tree. I watched the birds using their beaks to pluck fruit from the vines.

La hermosa casa de Pat

En la temporada seca, cuando refrescaba el aire, me gustaba asolearme en una roca arriba de la cascada. A veces dormía, pero con frecuencia solo descansaba en la belleza de la selva tropical. Un día varios tucanes estaban saltando a lo largo de las ramas de un árbol cercano, graznando "¡rrrk! ¡rrrk!" Sus pechos amarillos emplumados y sus picos de arco iris llenaba el árbol con color. Enredaderas de la fruta pasión envolvían el árbol. Yo miraba a los pájaros usando sus picos para arrancar a tirones la fruta de las enredaderas.

In our rainforest there are many beautiful creatures.

En nuestra selva tropical existen muchas hermosas criaturas.

The keel-billed toucan is the national bird of Belize.

El tucán es el pájaro nacional de Belice.

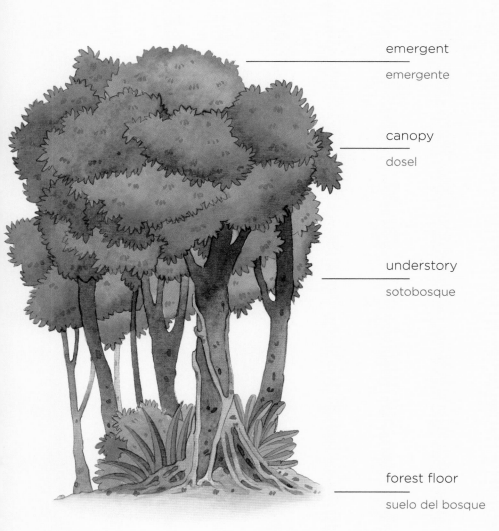

emergent

emergente

canopy

dosel

understory

sotobosque

forest floor

suelo del bosque

The rainforest has four levels: emergent, canopy, understory, and forest floor. The trees in the emergent layer can be up to 250 feet (76 meters) tall. The rainforest is hot and humid.

La selva tiene cuatro niveles: emergente, dosel, sotobosque y suelo del bosque. Los árboles en la capa emergente pueden medir hasta 250 pies (76 metros) de altura. La selva tropical es cálida y húmeda.

Jaguars live on the forest floor.

Los jaguares viven en el suelo del bosque.

Papaya (Papaya)

Orchid (Orquídea)

Tamarind (Tamarindo)

There are thousands of different kinds of plants and trees in the rainforests of Belize. Here are some of them:

Trees: Mahogany, cedar, sapodilla, ceiba, cohune palm, and fig

Plants: Ferns, orchids, and bromeliads

Fruit: Guava, tamarind, mango, and papaya

Hay miles de diferentes clases de plantas y árboles en la selva de Belice. Aquí algunos de ellos:
Árboles: Caoba, cedro, chicozapote, ceiba, palma de corozo e higo.
Plantas: Helechos, orquídeas y bromelias
Fruta: Guayaba, tamarindo, mango y papaya.

I heard a squeak and looked down to see a mother coati and four of her cubs emerge from the forest to drink. The mother coati sniffed the air nervously. Maybe she could smell me. My scent would mean danger to her, but she and her cubs were in no danger from me that day. I had already eaten and was enjoying a lazy afternoon in the sun. The coati family drank until they were satisfied. Then they disappeared into the underbrush.

Escuché un chillido y al mirar hacia abajo pude ver a una madre coatí y sus cuatro cachorros emerger de la selva buscando agua para beber. La madre coatí olfateó nerviosamente el aire. Quizá le sería posible olerme. Para ella, mi olor podría significar peligro, pero ella y sus cachorros no debían temerme ese día. Ya había comido y solo estaba gozando de una tarde soleada perezosa. La familia de coatíes bebió agua hasta que todos estuvieron satisfechos. Entonces desaparecieron dentro de la maleza.

Coati
Coatis are raccoon-like animals with long, ringed tails and long snouts.

Coatí
Los coatíes parecen mapaches, tiene largas colas anilladas y alargados hocicos.

29

I began traveling alone through my mother's territory. In my mind I carried a map of all the important places in my life. The map included the den we used when I was a just a cub. It also included the cave we slept in when I was bigger, the waterfall, the pool, and the place where I killed the peccary. I knew the location of every kill I had ever made.

I often walked along the borders of our territory. There I could see the tree trunks my mother had scratched to let other jaguars know this was our land. I could smell her scent markings, too. I often wondered what I might find in the forest beyond our territory.

By the time I was two years old, I was a powerful and skilled hunter. Male jaguars are solitary animals, and the day came when I needed to leave my mother's territory to find my own. My sister rubbed her cheeks against mine. My mother licked my face one last time. Then I ran off into the dark forest where I had never been before. I was on my own and ready for adventure.

Empecé a viajar solo por el territorio de mi madre. En mi mente tenía muy claro el mapa de todos los lugares que habían sido importantes en mi vida. El mapa incluía la guarida que usábamos cuando yo era tan solo un cachorro. También incluía la cueva donde dormíamos cuando fui más grande, la catarata, el estanque, y el lugar donde maté al pecarí. Sabía el lugar exacto de cada muerte que había yo hecho.

Con frecuencia caminaba a lo largo de los límites de nuestro territorio. Ahí podía ver los troncos que mi madre había rasguñado para que los otros jaguares supieran que ésta era nuestra tierra. Asimismo podía reconocer el olor de sus marcas. A menudo me preguntaba qué otras cosas podrían encontrarse más allá de nuestro territorio en la selva.

Cuando cumplí dos años, era ya un poderoso y hábil cazador. Los jaguares macho son animales solitarios, y llegó el día en que yo debí abandonar el territorio de mi madre y encontrar el mío propio. Por última vez mi hermana frotó su cachete contra el mío. Mi madre lamió mi cara. Entonces salí corriendo hacia dentro de la selva oscura donde nunca antes había estado. Iba solo y por mi cuenta, listo para la aventura.

Pat was growing in height, weight, and wisdom!

Pat estaba creciendo en altura, peso y sabiduría.

Jaguars stay with their mothers until they are two years old. At two they are adults and go off on their own.

Los jaguares se quedan con sus madres hasta que tienen dos años de edad. A los dos años son adultos y se van por su cuenta.

Solitary
Solitary means living alone.

Solitario
Solitario significa vivir solo.

CHAPTER 4

Pat on His Own

I had not traveled far when I came upon the scent of another jaguar. There were scratches on a large tree trunk, just like the markings my mother made. There was also a mound of leaves and fallen branches smelling strongly of jaguar urine. I moved on to explore but watched carefully in case the other jaguar was nearby.

I came to an opening in the forest, cut through by a wide river. I jumped in and swam just for the fun of it. A line of turtles, sunning themselves on a log, slid into the water, trying to hide from me. I easily caught one and cracked its shell. Then I settled down in a sunny spot along the shore to eat my lunch. A harpy eagle soared overhead. The curve of the river and even the air seemed new to me. I felt free and strong. I could take care of myself. The forest would give me all I needed.

Pat por su cuenta

No había viajado lejos cuando topé con el aroma de otro jaguar. Había rasguños en un gran tronco, justo como las marcas que había hecho mi madre. Había también un montón de hojas y ramas caídas en las cuales se percibía fuertemente el olor a orina del otro jaguar. Seguí explorando pero manteniéndome muy alerta en caso de que ese otro jaguar anduviera cerca.

Llegué a un claro en el bosque, dividido por un ancho río. Me metí de un brinco y nadé solo por diversión. Una fila de tortugas que se asoleaban sobre un tronco se lanzaron al agua, tratando de esconderse de mí. Fácilmente atrapé a una y partí su caparazón. Entonces me acomodé en un sitio asoleado en la orilla del río para comer mi almuerzo. Un águila arpía planeaba en las alturas. La curva del río e incluso el aire mismo parecían ser algo nuevo para mí. Me sentía libre y fuerte. Podía cuidarme yo solo. La selva me daría todo lo que necesitara.

The harpy eagle has a rear talon that can be as large as a grizzly bear paw.

El águila arpía posee una garra trasera que puede ser tan grande como la garra de un oso pardo.

Jaguars eat more than 85 different kinds of animals.

Los jaguares comen más de 85 diferentes clases de animales.

Suddenly, a fierce roar shook me, raising me to my feet. The biggest jaguar I had ever seen was bounding toward me. It was the jaguar who had marked the territory as his own, and he had come to defend it. His sharp teeth were bared, his huge shoulders hunched, and his head held low. Shaking, I roared back and showed him my own teeth. He jumped forward and swiped at me. I pulled back just in time to avoid the razor-sharp claws. I jumped at him, but he was bigger and stronger and too quick for me. He was an older, experienced fighter. I had wrestled my sister in play, but I had never defended myself in a real fight. The big cat was crouching for another attack when I turned and ran away as fast as I could. He crashed through the forest behind me. I never looked back as I ran.

After a while I could no longer hear him, and I slowed my pace. I began to notice an unpleasant smell. It grew stronger as I moved along. There was light up ahead that surely must mean a break in the trees around a river. I was thirsty and began to run again, hoping to find water.

De repente, un feroz rugido me sorprendió, haciéndome dar un brinco. El jaguar más grande que yo jamás hubiera visto en mi vida saltaba hacia mí. Era ese otro jaguar que había marcado ese territorio como suyo y ahora venía para defenderlo. Sus afilados dientes estaban al descubierto, sus enormes hombros encorvados y tenía la cabeza baja, listo para atacarme. Temblando le regresé el rugido y le enseñé mis dientes. Saltó hacia mí, golpeándome con fuerza. Me retiré justo a tiempo para evitar sus garras afiladas. Traté de saltarle encima, pero él era más grande y más fuerte y demasiado rápido para mí. Él era un luchador experimentado. Yo sólo había jugado a las luchas con mi hermana, pero nunca había tenido que defenderme en una pelea de verdad. El gran gato se encogió, listo para atacarme otra vez, pero yo giré y salí huyendo tan rápido como pude. Él se quedó rugiendo en el bosque detrás de mí. Mientras corría, yo nunca miré hacia atrás.

Después de un rato ya no podía oírlo, y frené un poco mi paso. Entonces empecé a notar un desagradable olor. Se hacía más fuerte a medida que yo avanzaba por la tupida selva. Una luz delante de mí me indicaba que existía un paso a través de los árboles alrededor del río. Tenía sed y volví a correr, esperando encontrar agua.

Jaguars are territorial. They defend their territories. They do not like it when other jaguars enter their space.

Los jaguares son territoriales. Defienden sus territorios. No les gustan cuando otros jaguares interrumpen su espacio.

Claws are a cat's secret weapon!

Las garras son el arma secreta del jaguar y de todos los felinos.

Jaguars scratch on logs and trees. They do this to mark their territories. It also keeps their nails healthy.

Los jaguares rasguñan los troncos de los árboles. Lo hacen para marcar su territorio. Además eso mantiene saludables sus uñas.

Jaguars are really neat animals. They are great American cats. We would not want a jaguar as a pet because it would eat us, but we still need to protect them in the wild!

Los jaguares son animales muy limpios. Son los grandes gatos americanos. No querríamos un jaguar como mascota porque nos comería, pero todavía tenemos que protegerlos en la naturaleza.

When you cut down the trees, you are cutting the home of the animals.

Cuando cortas los árboles, estás cortando la casa de los animales.

Jaguars are dying because people are destroying their habitats.

Los jaguares se están muriendo porque la gente está destruyendo su hábitat.

There was a clearing in the trees, but there was no river and no lagoon. There were no bushes, no birds, and no animals. A large stretch of the forest ahead of me was simply missing. I could see almost nothing green. Just brown dirt, scarred with deep ruts, and dotted with thousands of tree stumps. How did this happen? I could not make sense of this bare land.

Encontré ese claro entre los árboles del bosque. Pero no había río ni laguna. No había arbustos, pájaros ni animales. Una gran sección de la selva estaba totalmente perdida. Delante de mis ojos no podía encontrar nada que fuera verde. Solo veía la tierra herida con profundos surcos y salpicada con miles de troncos de árboles recién cortados. ¿Cómo sucedió esto? No podía encontrarle ningún sentido a esta selva vacía.

I had stumbled across a clear-cut section of the forest. Later I understood that humans had driven big machines into the forest and cut down the trees, carrying them away. The humans were loggers. They cut the trees into logs and sold them for money. At the time, I didn't know what logging was. I didn't know what humans were. I didn't understand money. How could I know that the people needed to sell the trees to buy food for their families? All I knew was the forest. I could survive an attack by another jaguar, but I didn't know if I could survive loggers taking away the forest.

I turned away from the **strange, bare land** and ran back into the green forest.

Más tarde, en ese bosque talado comprendí que los humanos habían traído maquinaria enorme a la selva tropical, habían cortado los árboles, y se los estaban llevando. Los humanos eran taladores. Ellos cortaban los árboles y vendían sus troncos por dinero. En ese momento, yo no sabía qué era la explotación forestal. No sabía qué eran los humanos. No entendía de dinero. ¿Cómo podía saber que la gente necesitaba cortar y vender los árboles para comprar comida para sus familias? Todo lo que yo conocía hasta entonces era la selva. En ella pude sobrevivir al ataque de otro jaguar, pero no sabía si podría sobrevivir a los taladores quitándome la selva.

Me fui de esa extraña tierra vacía de árboles y regresé corriendo a la frondosa selva verde.

Deforestation
Deforestation is the loss of forests due to overcutting of trees.

Deforestación
Deforestación es la pérdida de bosques debido a la tala excesiva de árboles.

Reasons for deforestation

- Farmers cut trees to clear land to grow food for their families.
- Loggers cut trees to sell the wood.
- Ranchers clear trees from the land so they can raise cattle to sell.
- Developers cut the trees to build roads, houses, and businesses.

People need houses for shelter; farms for food; and logging, ranches, and businesses to make money to live.

Razones para la deforestación

Los agricultores talan árboles para despejar la tierra y cultivar en granjas alimentos para sus familias.
- Los taladores cortan árboles para vender la madera.
- Los rancheros despejan de árboles la tierra para criar ganado y venderlo.
- Los urbanizadores cortan árboles para construir caminos, casas y negocios.

La gente necesita casas para refugiarse y granjas para cultivar su comida; necesita de la explotación forestal y de ranchos y negocios que les permita hacer dinero para vivir.

The Belize government is working to help slow down deforestation.

El gobierno de Belice está trabajando para ayudar a frenar la deforestación.

People from many countries buy wood from trees cut down in the forests of Belize.

Gente de muchos países compral la madera de árboles talados en la selva de Belice.

CHAPTER 5

Pat Claims His Territory

I roamed for days looking for land I could claim as my own territory. One day I came upon the markings of another jaguar, but the scent was old and faded. Maybe the jaguar was no longer living there. I sniffed the air. It smelled of fresh water, crocodiles, kinkajous, and mangos.

I explored the territory for several days. There was no other jaguar, and it was a good habitat. It had everything I needed to live. I found a dry cave to sleep in. There was no waterfall like the one in my mother's territory, but there was a river where I could fish. The forest was lush, providing cover for stalking prey.

Pat reclama su territorio

Vagué por días buscando tierras que pudiera reclamar como mí propio territorio. Un día me encontré con las marcas de otro jaguar, pero el olor que se desprendía de ella era viejo y débil. Quizás el jaguar no vivía más ahí. Olfateé el aire. Olía a agua fresca, a cocodrilos, mapaches y mangos.

Exploré el nuevo territorio por varios días. No había otro jaguar, y era un buen hábitat. Tenía todo lo que necesitaba para vivir. Encontré una cueva seca para dormir. No había cascada como en el territorio de mi madre, pero había un río donde podía pescar. El bosque era exuberante, proveía cubierta para acechar presas.

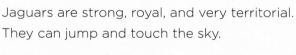

Jaguars are strong, royal, and very territorial. They can jump and touch the sky.

Los jaguares son fuertes, majestuosos, y muy territoriales. Cuando saltan, tocan el cielo.

Jaguars need a lot of land.

Los jaguares necesitan mucho terreno.

Habitat

A habitat is the natural place for an animal to live and grow. It is the animal's place in the environment.

Hábitat

El hábitat es un lugar natural para que vivan y crezcan los animales. Es el lugar de los animales en el medio ambiente.

Jaguars live in many different kinds of habitats: rainforests, swamps, savannas (grasslands), mountain scrub areas, and deciduous forests.

Los jaguares viven en diferentes clases de hábitats: selvas, pantanos, sabanas (praderas), áreas de maleza de la montaña y bosques efímeros.

Jaguar Territories

A male jaguar's territory is between 19 and 53 square miles (5,000 to 14,000 hectares). A female jaguar's territory is generally between 10 and 37 square miles (2,500 to 9,500 hectares).

Territorios de Jaguares

El territorio de un jaguar macho ocupa de 19 a 53 millas cuadradas (5,000 a 14,000 hectáreas). El territorio de un jaguar hembra ocupa generalmente de 10 a 37 millas cuadradas (2,5000 a 9,500 hectáreas).

There is a jaguar temple among the Maya ruins of Lamanai in Orange Walk, Belize. People believe there are still undiscovered Maya ruins in the forests of Belize.

Hay un templo del jaguar en Belice, entre las ruinas mayas de Lamanai en Orange Walk. La gente cree que aún hay ruinas mayas sin descubrir en la selva de Belice.

The Maya culture was the leading society in Central America from 1,500 B.C. to 500 A.D. Maya still live in Belize today.

La cultura maya era la sociedad líder en Centroamérica de 1,500 A.C al 500 D.C. Los mayas todavía viven hoy en Belice.

I began marking the boundaries of the territory with my scent to keep other jaguars out. One day I discovered something I had never seen before. An ancient Maya temple was hidden deep in the forest. Humans had built the pyramid of stone. It was surrounded by thick bushes. It was so covered with vines that I almost passed by without seeing it. Toucans were perched high on the temple, croaking in the sun. I was amazed to find the carving of a jaguar over one of the doorways. In the ancient Maya civilization, jaguars were thought to be gods. I looked at the jaguar carved in stone. I soared in my mind over the forest, back to the territory of my mother and my sister. I imagined them hunting and sunning themselves. How surprised they would be to see this ancient Maya temple, honoring the jaguar!

Empecé a marcar los límites del territorio con mi olor para que no entraran otros jaguares. Un día descubrí algo que nunca antes había visto. Un antiguo templo Maya estaba escondido en la profundidad del bosque. Los humanos habían construido la pirámide con piedras y estaba rodeada por espesos matorrales. Estaba tan cubierta de enredaderas que casi pasé junto a ella sin verla. Los tucanes estaban encaramados en lo alto del templo, cantando en el sol. Me sorprendí mucho al encontrar la talla de un jaguar sobre una de las puertas de la pirámide. En la antigua civilización maya, se creía que los jaguares eran dioses. Observé el jaguar tallado en la piedra. En mi mente remonté vuelo sobre el bosque tropical, de regreso al territorio de mi madre y de mi hermana. Las imaginé cazando y asoleándose. ¡Qué sorprendidas estarían de ver este antiguo templo maya, honrando al jaguar!

The Maya created a calendar, and a system of writing and of math. Their art was highly developed and they had an organized system of religion and of government.

Los Mayas crearon un calendario, y un sistema de escritura y de matemáticas. Su arte estaba muy desarrollado y tenían un sistema organizado de religión y de gobierno.

Ancient Maya Beliefs About Jaguars
- Jaguars are gods.
- Jaguars hold up the sky.
- Jaguar fur represents the stars in the night sky.
- Jaguars bring the sun in the morning and the moon at night.
- Jaguars are connected to the underworld because they often hunt at night.

Creencias de los antiguos mayas acerca de jaguares
- Los jaguares eran dioses.
- Los jaguares sostenían el cielo.
- La piel de los jaguares representaba las estrellas en el cielo nocturno.
- Los jaguares traían el sol en la mañana y la luna al anochecer.
- Los jaguares estaban conectados al mundo de los muertos porque son cazadores nocturnos.

CHAPTER 6

Pat is Injured

I spent years in my territory. I lived a solitary life, but at times I wandered long distances to find a female jaguar. Other times I roamed many miles away from home looking for prey. Back in my territory, I used to climb the Maya pyramid and stretch out on the step above the jaguar doorway in the moonlight. One night, a dusty brown tapir wandered below me. I did not often see tapirs because people had hunted so many of them that there were not many left in the forest.

Pat se lesiona

Pasé muchos años en mi territorio. Viví una vida solitaria, a veces anduve largas distancias para encontrar a un jaguar hembra. Otras veces vagaba muchas millas lejos de casa buscando presas. De regreso en mi territorio, acostumbraba trepar la pirámide maya y descansar en el escalón arriba de la puerta del jaguar en el claro de luna. Una noche, un tapir color café cenizo vagaba cerca de mí. No veía tapires con frecuencia porque la gente había cazado tantos que ya no quedaban muchos de ellos en el bosque.

The tapir is the national animal of Belize.

El tapir es el animal nacional de Belice.

Jaguars aren't eaten by other animals.

Los jaguares no son comidos por otros animales.

Humans hunt some of the same animals jaguars hunt. This is making it harder for jaguars to find enough prey to eat.

Los humanos cazan algunos de los mismos animales que los jaguares cazan. Esto está haciendo más difícil para los jaguares encontrar suficientes presas para comer.

Jaguars are loners.
They do not live in groups.

Los jaguares son solitarios.
No viven en grupos.

I crouched and crept slowly along the step, watching the tapir carefully.
I leapt from my perch to a lower step on the pyramid closer to the
animal. My aim was sure and I landed securely, but the ancient stone was rotten. It crumbled under my weight. I fell, hitting my hind leg on a stone below. Pain shot up my leg and into my hip. I roared and saw the frightened tapir run for cover.

I lay on the forest floor. My leg was broken. There was no doctor to help me. No medicine, no operation, no cast. There was no one to feed me or bring me water. I couldn't run. I couldn't climb. I couldn't leap to attack my prey.
How would I survive?

Me agaché y deslicé lentamente por el escalón, observando cuidadosamente al tapir. Salté de mi posición a un escalón más bajo en la pirámide para quedar más cerca del animal. Desde ahí consideré que mi objetivo estaba asegurado y que aterrizaría en forma segura sobre el tapir, pero caí sobre una antigua piedra que se pulverizó con mi peso. Al caer sobre la piedra me lastimé mi pata trasera. El dolor corrió por mi pata y llegó hasta la cadera. Rugí de dolor y vi al asustado tapir correr a resguardarse.

Me eché en el suelo del bosque. Mi pata estaba rota. No había doctor que me ayudara. Estaba sin medicinas, sin cirugía, sin yeso. No había nadie que me diera de comer o me trajera agua. No podía correr. No podía trepar. No podía saltar sobre ninguna presa. ¿Cómo sobreviviría?

It is important for people to know that jaguars are a good part of our world. It would be sad if they weren't around anymore.

Es importante que la gente sepa que los jaguares son una buena parte de nuestro mundo. Sería triste si ellos no estuvieran más aquí.

When a jaguar in the wild becomes sick or injured, it usually dies because it cannot protect itself and cannot hunt for food to survive.

Cuando un jaguar en la naturaleza se enferma o lastima, usualmente muere porque no puede protegerse y no puede cazar comida para sobrevivir.

I tried to limp toward my cave,

but it was too far to travel with my wounded leg. I dragged myself to the jaguar doorway and lay down to rest. I spent many days there in the shade of the Maya temple. It was the rainy season, and I was able to drink from the puddles that formed each day. I fed on the kind of prey my mother had first taught me to hunt—small iguanas, mice, and birds. I brought down these animals with one swat of my paw.

Even with these meals, I couldn't get enough to eat. ## I grew thin and weak. I slept often and ate whatever I could catch, but many days I went hungry. My leg was healing slowly. Weeks later, I was able to walk again. I limped the miles back through the forest to my cave. Along the way I stopped to rest in the cool river that ran through my territory. It was wonderful to lap up all I wanted of the fresh, clear water after so many weeks of drinking only from rain puddles.

Traté de regresar cojeando hacia mi cueva, pero estaba demasiado lejos para llegar con mi pata lastimada. Me arrastré entonces hasta la pirámide maya y me eché frente a la puerta del jaguar para descansar. Pasé muchos días ahí, a la sombra del templo maya. Era la temporada de lluvias, y pude tomar agua de los charcos que se formaban cada día. Me alimenté solo con la clase de presas que mi madre me enseñó a casar primero, iguanas, ratones y pájaros. Cazaba a estos animales de un fuerte zarpazo.

Pero incluso con estas comidas, no encontraba lo suficiente para sustentarme. Me puse flaco y débil. Estando así, dormía mucho, comía sólo lo que podía atrapar a zarpazos. Muchos días pasé hambre. Mi pata sanaba muy lentamente. Semanas después, pude volver a caminar. Cojeé millas para regresar a mi cueva a través del bosque tropical. Por el camino me paraba a descansar en el río fresco que corría hasta llegar a mi territorio. Fue maravilloso beber todo lo que quería de agua fresca y clara después de tantas semanas de haber estado bebiendo únicamente de los charcos que se formaban con la lluvia.

Belize has two seasons.

Dry Season

| December | January | February |
| March | April | May |

Wet Season

| June | July | August |
| September | October | November |

Belice tiene dos estaciones.

Temporada seca

| Diciembre | Enero | Febrero |
| Marzo | Abril | Mayo |

Temporada húmeda

| Junio | Julio | Agosto |
| Septiembre | Octubre | Noviembre |

CHAPTER 7

Pat Discovers Cattle

Even though my leg healed, it was much weaker than before it was broken. Many times I would leap to attack a crocodile or a deer only to find I was too slow. The crocodile would sink to the safety of deeper water, or the deer would dart into the forest. I caught enough prey to stay alive, but I was constantly hungry.

When I regained my strength, I walked all the way around the borders of my territory, leaving fresh scent marks to keep away any jaguars who might try to take my land from me. One evening I finally reached the farthest edge of my territory. There I smelled a familiar unpleasant odor. It was the same scent I had smelled long ago at the clear-cut forest. I turned to leave, but **I caught the scent of new prey.** My mouth watered. I sat for a long time sniffing the air and looking for signs of danger. Finally my hunger pushed me onward.

Pat descubre el ganado

Aún cuando mi pata se curó, yo estaba más débil que antes que se rompiera. Muchas veces me arrastraba para atacar a un cocodrilo o a un venado, solo para descubrir que yo era demasiado lento. El cocodrilo se sumergía velozmente a la seguridad del agua profunda y el venado salía disparado al bosque. Cacé suficientes presas para sobrevivir, pero constantemente tenía hambre.

Cuando recobré mi fuerza, caminé hasta llegar a los límites de mi territorio, dejando marcas con mi olor fresco que alejarían a cualquier jaguar que quisiera tratar de robarme mi tierra. Una tarde finalmente llegué al borde más lejano de mi territorio. Estando ahí percibí un olor conocido y desagradable. Era el mismo aroma que hacía mucho tiempo detecté en el bosque talado. Di la vuelta para irme pero entonces llegó hasta mí el aroma de una nueva presa. Se me hizo agua la boca. Me senté olfateando el aire por mucho tiempo, buscando señales de peligro. Finalmente el hambre me puso en movimiento.

Sometimes ranchers hunt jaguars to stop them from killing their cattle.

A veces los ganaderos cazan jaguares para evitar que éstos maten su ganado.

As I drew closer to the prey, I could see that many trees had been cut down, and there were buildings that hadn't been there before. I also saw the new prey: cattle. Ranchers had cleared the trees to raise cattle for money to help make life better for their families. Several dozen cattle were roaming lazily in the clearing near the forest. I had never seen such animals before. They were very big, but maybe I could take one down.

A medida que iba acercándome a la presa, noté que muchos árboles habían sido talados y que había construcciones que antes no existían. También descubrí una nueva presa: el ganado. Los rancheros habían talado los árboles para criar ganado por dinero, así lograban tener una vida mejor para sus familias. Varias docenas de reses se paseaban perezosamente en el claro talado del bosque. Nunca antes había visto a tales animales. Eran muy grandes, pero tal vez podría cazar uno.

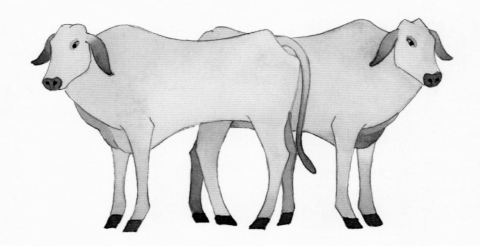

The cattle bellowed nervously as I slinked along the edge of the forest. They moved away from me, huddling together, but one steer didn't move as quickly as the others. **I pounced.** That night I ate my first full meal since I had broken my leg. This was my first taste of beef. It was delicious.

I left the carcass where it lay. It was too big to drag with my damaged leg. That night in my cave, I dreamed of a sea of cattle, each steer fatter than the next. In my dream I ate and ate and ate until my belly filled like a balloon. Still dreaming, I floated away, high above the rainforest to a strange land where I was surrounded by strange animals.

El ganado bramó nerviosamente mientras me escabullía por el borde del bosque. Las reses se alejaban de mí, agrupándose, pero un novillo no se movió tan rápido como los otros. Me le abalancé. Esa noche comí mi primera cena completa desde que me rompí la pata. Ese fue mi primer bocado de res. Fue delicioso.

Dejé tirado el esqueleto de la res. Era demasiado grande para arrastrarlo hasta mi guarida teniendo la pata herida. Esa noche, en mi cueva, soñé con un mar de ganado, cada novillo más gordo que el siguiente. En mi sueño comí, comí y comí hasta que mi estómago se llenaba como un globo. Todavía soñando, flotaba por lo alto de la selva hacia una tierra extraña donde eme rodeaban animales extraños.

Since the trees were cut down,
Pat snacked on the farmer's cattle.

Desde que talaron los árboles, Pat comía
su botana en el ganado.

A healthy jaguar can drag the body of a 1,200 pound (545 kilogram) steer.

Un jaguar sano puede arrastrar el cuerpo de un novillo de 1,200 libras (545 kilogramos)

CHAPTER 8

Pat is Captured

The next day I felt energized by the full meal I had eaten. As the day went on, I found myself thinking about the steer I had killed. I knew it would still be where I had left it. Even if another animal had eaten some of it, there would still be plenty left for me.

My hunger grew.
At sunset I headed back toward the cattle. Their scent grew stronger as I neared the ranch. The other scent, the one that made my fur tingle, was there too, but I would be careful. I had done this before.

Cattle bellowed and scattered as I slipped through the trees. I looked around, but I couldn't find the animal I had killed. Where could it be? I darted at the cattle, scattering them again so I could see the ground where they were standing. The steer I had killed was nowhere to be seen.

Pat es capturado

Al día siguiente tenía mucha energía por la comida completa que había ingerido. A medida que pasaba el día, me encontré pensando acerca del novillo que había matado. Yo sabía que todavía estaría donde lo había dejado. Incluso si otro animal hubiera comido algo, habría aún lo suficiente para mí.

Mi hambre creció. Al atardecer me dirigí nuevamente hacía el ganado. Su olor se hacía más fuerte mientras más me acercaba al rancho. El otro aroma, el que hacía que mi piel hormigueara de horror, también estaba ahí, pero tendría cuidado. Ya antes había hecho esto.

El ganado bramó y se dispersó mientras yo me deslizaba a través de los árboles. Miré alrededor, pero no podía encontrar al animal que había matado. ¿Dónde podría estar? Me lancé al ganado, dispersándolo otra vez para así poder ver el suelo que pisaban. No veía por ningún lado al novillo que había matado.

People should not kill jaguars.

La gente no debería matar jaguares.

The farmer must have thought,
"What in the world is happening here?"

El ganadero debe haber pensado
"¿Qué diablos está pasando aquí?"

Then a light blinded me, and I heard a deafening BANG! The sound launched me out of the clearing. I raced toward the dark forest. As I ran, I heard someone shouting, "Don't shoot! Don't shoot!"

And then came another voice, "But he's killing our cattle! How will we feed our children if that jaguar takes our animals?" I heard no more. I was speeding through the underbrush of the rainforest to the safety of my cave.

Entonces una luz me cegó y oí un ensordecedor ¡BANG! El sonido me mandó corriendo fuera del bosque talado. Corrí hacia el bosque oscuro. Mientras corría, oí a alguien gritando, "¡No disparen!" "¡No disparen!"

Y luego oí otra voz, "¡Pero está matando a nuestro ganado!" "¿Cómo alimentaremos a nuestros niños si ese jaguar se lleva nuestros animales?" No oí más. Iba corriendo a alta velocidad a través de la maleza de la selva para llegar a la seguridad de mi cueva.

I spent the next several days hunting small prey. I tried for a deer and stalked a herd of peccaries, but I had no luck. I tried to satisfy my hunger with frogs and turtles, but they never filled me up. After another two days, my hunger overcame my fear, and I made my way back toward the cattle. It was night.

I moved slowly in the darkness. I paced silently at the edge of the forest, looking out at the cattle for signs of danger. The cattle were calm. The foul odor was there, but not as strong as last time. Then I noticed a new scent, another kind of prey.

Los días siguientes, los pasé cazando pequeñas presas. Traté de atrapar un venado y también aceché a una manada de pecaríes, pero no tuve suerte. Intenté satisfacer mi hambre con ranas y tortugas, pero nunca me saciaba. Después de dos días de comer poco, el hambre que sentía superó mi miedo y tomé el camino de regreso hacia el ganado. Era de noche.

Me movía lentamente en la oscuridad. Caminé en silencio al borde del bosque, mirando atentamente al ganado para descubrir señales de peligro. El ganado estaba en calma. El mal olor continuaba ahí, pero no era tan fuerte como la vez anterior. Entonces noté un nuevo aroma, otra clase de presa.

Jaguars are very quiet when they are stalking their prey.

Los jaguares son muy silenciosos cuando están acechando su presa.

People need to provide for their families, and jaguars need wild places to live where they can be healthy.

La gente necesita mantener a sus familias y los jaguares necesitan lugares naturales para vivir donde puedan ser saludables.

I followed my nose. Something was there between the cattle and me. I could see a fat animal, about the size of a young peccary. It was a small farm pig, standing still among rows of thin, straight branches. The cattle were tempting, but I remembered the terrible gunshot and the shouting the last time I ran among the cattle.

I crept up on the pig. It did not run. I leapt. The moment I landed, **I was startled by a clanging noise,** and I jumped back. I crashed into the strange branches. They were hard and unbending. They were not branches at all. They were metal bars.

Seguí a mi nariz. Algo estaba ahí, entre el ganado y yo. Podía ver a un animal gordo, como del tamaño de un pecarí joven. Era un cerdito de rancho, detenido entre filas de ramas muy delgadas y rectas. Esa presa era tentadora, pero recordé el terrible disparo y los gritos de la última vez que corrí entre el ganado.

Me acerqué sigilosamente al cerdo. No corrió. Yo salté. En el momento que caí, me sobresaltó un ruido metálico, di un brinco hacia atrá,s pero me estrellé en las extrañas ramas. Eran duras y no se doblaban. No eran en absoluto ramas. Eran barras de metal.

Panthera is an organization that works to conserve (save) wild cats, including jaguars.

Panthera es una organización que trabaja para conservar (salvar) gatos salvajes, incluyendo jaguares.

The Belize government and Panthera are teaching ranchers new ways to manage their ranches without killing jaguars.

El gobierno de Belice y Panthera están enseñando a los ganaderos nuevas formas de administrar sus ranchos sin matar jaguares.

Jaguar jaws are stronger than the jaws of any other cat in the world.

Las mandíbulas del jaguar son más fuertes que las mandíbulas de cualquier otro felino en el mundo.

Pat must have been so scared that he thought it was his last day.

Pat debió estar tan asustado que pensó que ése era su último día.

I looked around and saw I was **trapped in a cage.** The pig had been bait. I threw my weight against the bars but could not escape. I roared and began biting the bars. I could not break out. I continued to bite down as hard as I could, but my jaws were not strong enough. I could hear my teeth cracking against the bars. Pain shot through my face. I finally gave up.

Miré alrededor y vi que estaba atrapado en una jaula. El cerdo había sido la carnada para atraparme. Aventé mi cuerpo contra las barras pero no conseguía escapar. Rugí y empecé a morder las barras. No podía salir. Continué mordiendo tanto como podía pero mis mandíbulas no eran lo suficientemente fuertes. Podía escuchar mis dientes rompiéndose contra las barras. Ráfagas de dolor corrieron por mi cara. Finalmente cedí.

CHAPTER 9

Pat Gets Help

When the sun rose in the morning, I saw the animals with the unpleasant scent. Humans. I clawed the bars and roared at them as they lifted me into the back of a pickup truck.

I bumped for an hour over dirt roads in the back of the truck. Not only had I never seen people before, I had never seen a car, a truck, a town, or anything human except the small buildings of the cattle ranch. I was confused.

Pat recibe ayuda

Cuando el sol salió en la mañana, vi a los animales de olor desagradable. Los humanos. Rasguñé las barras y les rugí mientras levantaban la jaula donde estaba preso y la colocaban en la parte trasera de la camioneta.

Reboté durante una hora por los caminos de tierra en la parte trasera de la camioneta. No sólo no había visto gente nunca antes, tampoco había visto jamás un carro, una camioneta, un pueblo o cualquier cosa humana, excepto por las pequeñas construcciones del rancho de ganado. Me sentía muy confundido.

Mexico

Honey Camp
Lagoon

Guatemala

Belize Zoo
X

Belize

Caribbean Sea

We stopped at a place called Honey Camp Lagoon in Orange Walk, Belize, where the people found a dentist to take care of my teeth. The dentist did his best, but my teeth were so badly damaged I would never be able to survive in the rainforest. I didn't know what I would do.

The people at Honey Camp Lagoon had heard that the government of Belize helped jaguars like me. They called the Forest Department, who sent someone to get me. The government people took me to the Belize Zoo. The Belize Zoo had a Problem Jaguar Rehabilitation Program to help jaguars that were injured, or had come into repeated conflict with humans and thus were unable to be returned to the wild.

Nos detuvimos en un lugar llamado Honey Camp Lagoon en Orange Walk, Belice, donde la gente encontró a un dentista para que se ocupara de mis dientes. El dentista hizo lo mejor que pudo, pero mis dientes estaban tan dañados que nunca sería capaz de sobrevivir en la selva. No sabía lo que haría.

La gente de Honey Camp Lagoon había oído que el gobierno de Belice ayudaba a los jaguares como yo. Hablaron al Departamento del Bosque, quien envió a alguien para recogerme. La gente del gobierno me llevó al Zoológico de Belice El Zoológico de Belice tenía un Programa de Rehabilitación para Jaguares en Problemas para ayudar a jaguares que estuvieran heridos, o que hubieran tenido conflictos repetido con los humanos, por lo que no podían ser regresados a su hábitat natural.

Imagine how you would feel if you had never even seen a truck, and suddenly you were tossed into the back of some loud, vibrating contraption. Yikes!

Imagina como te sentirías si nunca hubieras visto un camión y, de repente, fueras aventado en la parte trasera de un aparato ruidoso y vibrador. ¡Huy!

Losing their habitats is one of the biggest threats to jaguars.

La pérdida de sus hábitats es una de las mayores amenazas para los jaguares.

Before I arrived at the Belize Zoo, I had no idea how many jaguars were in trouble. Like me, they found humans coming into their territories for logging or farming. Some humans were hunting jaguars with guns. Some humans were hunting the same animals that jaguars hunt, leaving less food for us.

Jaguars need to travel long distances to find mates, to hunt, and to find new territories. It is confusing and dangerous for jaguars to travel through land used by humans.

Antes de llegar al Zoológico de Belice, no tenía idea de cuántos jaguares estaban en problemas. Como yo, ellos encontrar en su territorio a humanos dedicados a la explotación forestal y la agricultura. Algunos humanos estaban cazando jaguares con pistolas. Algunos humanos cazaban los mismos animales que los jaguares cazan, dejándonos con menos comida.

Los jaguares necesitan viajar grandes distancias para encontrar pareja, cazar y para encontrar nuevos territorios. Es confuso y peligroso para los jaguares viajar a través de la tierra que los humanos trabajan.

The Belize government and Panthera are working to save jaguar habitats. In 2010 they created a 7,000-acre (2,800-hectare) jaguar corridor called the Labouring Creek Jaguar Corridor, midway between Belize City and the capital city, Belmopan.

El gobierno de Belice y Panthera están trabajando para salvar los hábitats de los jaguares. En el año 2010 crearon un corredor de 7,000 acres (2,800 hectáreas) para los jaguares, llamado Labouring Creek Jaguar Corridor, a mitad del camino entre la ciudad de Belice y Belmopan, ciudad capital de Belice.

Jaguars hunt over huge areas. That is why we people need to protect large tracts of forest.

Los jaguares cazan en áreas enormes. Ese es el motivo por el cual nosotros, la gente, necesitamos proteger grandes extensiones del bosque.

The country of Belize helps jaguars. The Cockscomb Basin Wildlife Sanctuary in Belize was the first jaguar preserve in the world. The preserve saves natural habitats for jaguars to live and travel in. Panthera also helps jaguars. Panthera is working with governments to save corridors of land for the jaguars. The corridors are stretches of wild habitat that serve as trails or passages. Jaguars can roam long distances through the corridors to find their own territories, prey, or mates.

El país de Belice ayuda a los jaguares. El Cockscomb Basin Wildlife Sanctuary en Belice fue la primera reserva para jaguares en el mundo. Esta reserva salva hábitats naturales para que los jaguares vivan y viajen. Panthera está trabajando con los gobiernos para salvar corredores de tierra para los jaguares. Los corredores son tramos de hábitat silvestre que sirven como senderos o pasajes. Los jaguares pueden desplazarse largas distancias largas a través de lestos corredores para encontrar sus propios territorios, sus presas o sus parejas.

Jaguars are no longer able to live on 40% of the land they used to roam.

Los jaguares ya no pueden vivir en un 40% de la tierra que acostumbraban recorrer.

Jaguars used to live in Texas, Arizona, and New Mexico in the United States, but they don't live there anymore.

Antes los jaguares vivían en Texas, Arizona y Nuevo México en los Estados Unidos, pero ya no.

Jaguars are already extinct in the countries of El Salvador and Uruguay.

Los jaguares ya se han extinguido en los países de El Salvador y Uruguay.

CHAPTER 10

Pat at the Belize Zoo

When I arrived at the Belize Zoo, I smelled many animals, more than I had ever smelled in one place at the same time. Among them I smelled jaguars.

The people took me to the forested area behind the zoo and let me go in a patch of forest surrounded by a tall chain link fence. I ran through the ferns and bushes and quickly climbed a tree. The other jaguars were in their own patches of forest right next to mine. We were kept apart by metal fences. During my first days there, I spent a lot of time watching the other jaguars, growling at them and showing them how big I was.

Pat en el Zoológico de Belice

Cuando llegué al zoológico de Belice, olí muchos animales, más de los que había olido en un solo lugar al mismo tiempo. Entre ellos olí jaguares.

La gente me llevó al área boscosa detrás del zoológico y me dejaron en una parcela del bosque rodeada de una reja alta de alambre. Corrí a través de los arbustos y rápidamente me trepé a un árbol. Los otros jaguares estaban en sus propias parcelas junto a la mía. Nos tenían separados por rejas metálicas. Durante mi primer día ahí, pasé mucho tiempo observando a los otros jaguares, gruñéndoles y mostrándoles lo grande y poderoso que yo era.

Pat had to get used to having other animals living close to him in the zoo.

Pat se tenía que acostumbrar a tener a otros animales viviendo cerca de él en el zoológico.

If in the future you have a child or two, take them for a walk at the Belize Zoo.

Si en el futuro tienes un hijo o dos, llévalos a un paseo al zoológico de Belice.

The Problem Jaguar Rehabilitation Program was started at the Belize Zoo in 2004.

El Programa de Rehabilitación de Jaguares en Problemas inició en Belice en 2004.

The Problem Jaguar Rehabilitation Program at the Belize Zoo helps jaguars that can't go back into the wild. It feeds them, gives them medical care, and helps jaguars adjust to a new life that includes humans.

El Programa de Rehabilitación de Jaguares en problemas en el zoológico de Belice ayuda a los jaguares que no pueden regresar a la naturaleza. Los alimenta, le da atención médica y ayuda a los jaguares a adaptarse a una nueva vida que incluye a los humanos.

A woman with curly, red hair slid food to me through a small opening in my fence. There was a man with black hair who helped her. They fed me and gave me a large pan of water to drink each day. At first they came and went quickly, and I stayed far away from them. Then they started to spend more time near me each day. They talked to me in gentle voices. **They sang to me.** Sometimes I walked close to them along the inside of my fence. When I smelled their scent, I would run to see if they were bringing me food.

Una mujer con cabello rizado y pelirrojo me deslizaba comida a través de una pequeña abertura en mi reja. Había un hombre de cabello negro que le ayudaba. Ellos me alimentaron y me dieron una gran vasija para beber agua a diario. Al principio llegaban y se iban rápidamente, y yo me quedaba alejado de ellos. Entonces empezaron a pasar más tiempo cerca de mi cada día. Me hablaban con voces gentiles. Me cantaban. A veces caminaba cerca de ellos por la parte interior de mi reja. Cuando olía su aroma, corría para ver si me traían comida.

People should conserve jaguars. They are important.

La gente debería proteger a los jaguares. Ellos son importantes.

I know I want to rescue jaguars.

Sé que quiero rescatar jaguares.

After I was in the rehabilitation program for a while, a female jaguar arrived. She was named Springfield to honor the community whose people saved her life. Springfield was pregnant, but she was also very sick. Soon she gave birth to **a cub that people named Junior Buddy,** but she was too sick to care for him. So the gentle man in charge of all of the animals took care of Springfield and helped to make her well. The people who cared for us took care of Junior Buddy and kept him safe and warm.

When Junior Buddy was bigger, he was put in a space next to mine. Junior's mother was still sick and not able to teach him how to be a jaguar, so I spent time every day showing him what he needed to know. He would watch me through the fence that divided us. I taught him how to lick his fur to keep it clean. I taught him how to stalk prey. We practiced pouncing on butterflies and other insects.

Después de que estuve por un tiempo en el programa de rehabilitación, una hembra jaguar llegó. La llamaron Springfield para honrar a la gente de la comunidad que le había salvado la vida. Springfield estaba preñada y también muy enferma. Pronto tuvo a su cachorro al que la gente llamó Junior Buddy, pero ella estaba demasiado enferma para cuidarlo. De manera que el hombre gentil a cargo de todos los animales cuidó a Springfield y la ayudó para que se recuperara. La gente que nos cuidaba a nosotros también cuidó a Junior Buddy y lo mantuvo seguro y caliente.

Cuando Junior Buddy era más grande, lo pusieron en un espacio junto al mío. La madre de Junior todavía estaba enferma y no era capaz de enseñarle cómo ser un jaguar, así que cada día yo pasaba tiempo enseñándole lo que necesitaba saber. Él me miraba a través de la reja que nos dividía. Le enseñé cómo lamer su piel para mantenerla limpia. Le enseñé cómo acechar una presa. Practicamos abalanzándonos sobre mariposas y otros insectos.

Pat had to adjust to living in a closed-in space instead of his large territory in the wild.

Pat tuvo que adaptarse a vivir en un espacio cerrado en vez de en su gran territorio en la naturaleza.

At night when the people were gone, small animals called agoutis visited the zoo. They walked along the pathways looking for food people might have dropped during the day. Sometimes Junior Buddy and I would stalk the agoutis even though we couldn't get to them through the fence. Junior would crouch low and creep slowly with his tail swishing back and forth. Then just as an agouti passed by, he would leap. The startled agouti would jump and run away.

Over time I got used to the other jaguars in their enclosures so close to me. At night we would call to each other in the moonlight. Junior Buddy learned to join us with his young voice. Sometimes jaguars living in the forest close to the zoo would call out to answer us, and I would dream of my life in the wild.

Por la noche, cuando la gente se había ido, pequeños animales llamados tuzas visitaban el zoológico. Caminaban a lo largo de los caminos buscando comida que le gente hubiera dejado caer durante el día. A veces Junior Buddy y yo acechábamos a las tuzas aun cuando no podíamos agarrarlas a través de la reja. Junior se agachaba deslizándose lentamente moviendo la cola de aquí para allá. Entonces justo cuando una tuza pasaba nosotros saltábamos. La tuza sorprendida brincaba y huía.

Con el tiempo me acostumbré a los otros jaguares en sus jaulas muy cercanas a la mía. En la noche, nos llamábamos uno al otro a la luz de la luna. Junior Buddy aprendió a unirse a nosotros con su voz joven. Algunas veces, los jaguares que viven en el bosque cercano al zoológico nos respondían. Yo soñaba con mi vida en la naturaleza.

One day a couple, a man and a woman, came to see me. I had never seen them before. They began talking to me in low voices. My muscles tensed as they talked. I swished my tail. I growled loudly and jumped on the fence with my front legs high and wide and my sharp claws extended.

They continued talking to me in gentle voices. I paced back and forth. I did what I could to make myself look big. Finally, when it seemed they were not going to do anything to hurt me, I lay down not far from them. They spent a lot of time with me, feeding me bits of food by hand, and sometimes just sitting in the sun, listening to the sounds of the forest with me. They often came to visit me, and I became used to having them around.

Un día una pareja, un hombre y una mujer, vinieron a verme. Nunca antes los había visto. Empezaron a hablarme con voz baja. Mis músculos se tensaban mientras hablaban. Moví mi cola. Rugí con fuerza y brinqué en la reja con mis patas delanteras extendidas y abiertas, mis garras extendidas.

Continuaron hablándome con voz amable, Caminaba de un lado a otro. Hacía lo que podía para lucir grande. Finalmente, cuando parecía que no iban a hacer nada para herirme, me eché no lejos de ellos. Pasaron mucho tiempo conmigo, dándome bocados de comida con la mano y a veces solos sentados a la par mía, oyendo conmigo los sonidos del bosque. Con frecuencia venían a visitarme y me acostumbré a tenerlos alrededor.

Zoos are important. The animals there are cared for by people who really love them.

Los zoológicos son importantes. Los animales de ahí son cuidados por gente que realmente los ama.

I have learned that life is always changing and it doesn't always seem fair. New neighborhoods can seem scary at first, even when you are a jaguar. But one thing I have come to know for sure is that it is very helpful to have friends. The zoo lady, the man with the black hair, the gentle man in charge of the animals and the couple in Belize all helped me get used to having humans as neighbors. Even though I would roar at them from time to time, their voices, the games they played with me, and the gentle way they gave me food made a tough situation, well, not so bad. I even learned that other jaguars weren't too bad to be around in this new life, as long as they kept their distance.

He aprendido que la vida está cambiando siempre y no siempre parece justa. Al principio pueden dar miedo los lugares nuevos, aún cuando eres un jaguar. Pero una cosa he aprendido con certeza, que es de gran ayuda tener amigos. La dama del zoológico, el hombre de pelo negro, el hombre amable a cargo de los animales y la pareja en Belice me ayudaron a acostumbrarme a tener a los humanos como vecinos. Aún cuando les gruñía de vez en vez, sus voces, los juegos que jugaban conmigo y la manera gentil en que me daban comida hicieron una situación difícil, no tan mala. Incluso aprendí que no era tan grave estar alrededor de otros jaguares en esta vida nueva, siempre y cuando mantuvieran su distancia.

It took several years for Pat to learn to trust people, but Pat is still a wild animal.

Le tomó varios años a Pat aprender a confiar en la gente, pero Pat sigue siendo un animal salvaje.

What I didn't know then was that the people who cared for me knew that **I was an important jaguar.** They knew I needed to move to a new home to do a very important job in a new country far away.

Lo que no sabía entonces era que la gente que me cuidaba sabía que yo era un jaguar importante. Sabían que necesitaba mudarme a una casa nueva para hacer un trabajo muy importante en un país lejano.

CHAPTER 11

Pat Journeys to a New Life

When the people at the rehabilitation program decided I was ready, they made arrangements for me to fly in an airplane all the way to my new home at the Milwaukee County Zoo in Wisconsin, U.S.A. They prepared a large crate for me to travel in. It was hard for me to understand what was happening. I didn't know when they put me on the airplane, that **I would never see my forest home again.**

I could hear the roar of the engine and feel the bumps as we flew through choppy air. It was dark in my crate. I didn't even know I was flying through the sky. I tried to understand what was happening using my sense of smell. There was no scent of fresh rain, tapir, coati, or other jaguars. **Everything smelled strange.** Finally I fell asleep. I awoke as the plane landed.

Pat viaja a una vida nueva

Cuando la gente del programa de rehabilitación decidió que yo estaba listo, hicieron arreglos para que volara en un avión hasta mi nuevo hogar en el zoológico del condado de Milwaukee en Winsconsin, EE.UU. Prepararon una gran caja para que yo viajara. Era difícil para mí entender qué estaba pasando. Cuando me pusieron en el avión no sabía que nunca más volvería a ver mi hogar en el bosque otra vez.

Podía escuchar el zumbido del motor y sentir los golpes mientras volamos a través del aire variable. Estaba oscuro en mi cajón. Ni siquiera sabía que estaba volando por el cielo. Traté de comprender que estaba pasando utilizando mi sentido del olfato. No había olor a lluvia fresca, tapires, coatíes u otro jaguar. Todo olía extraño. Finalmente me quedé dormido. Desperté mientras el avión aterrizaba.

I can now say I know about flying cats!

¡Ahora puedo decir que sé de gatos voladores!

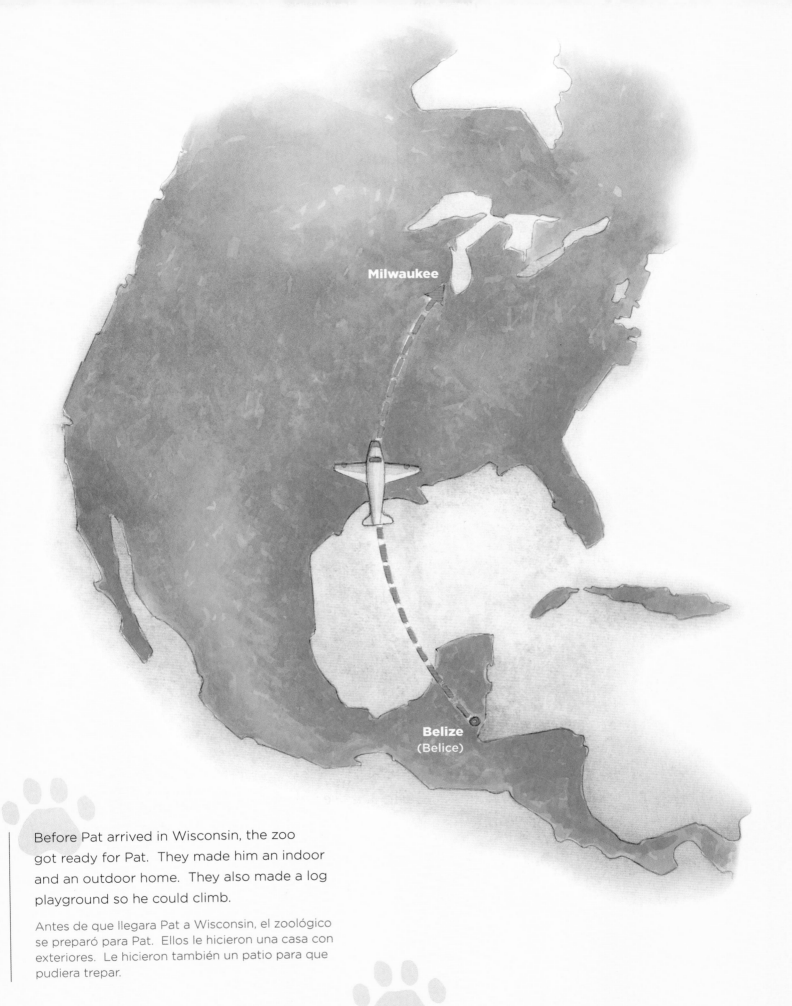

Milwaukee

Belize
(Belice)

Before Pat arrived in Wisconsin, the zoo got ready for Pat. They made him an indoor and an outdoor home. They also made a log playground so he could climb.

Antes de que llegara Pat a Wisconsin, el zoológico se preparó para Pat. Ellos le hicieron una casa con exteriores. Le hicieron también un patio para que pudiera trepar.

Pat arrived at the Milwaukee County Zoo on March 18, 2008.

Pat llegó al zoológico del condado de Milwaukee el 18 de marzo de 2008.

People were excited about my arrival in Milwaukee. To them I meant hope for the future of jaguars. It's hard for jaguars in zoos to find mates because so many are from the same family. If a male and a female jaguar from the same family have cubs together, their cubs can be weak and often sickly. To solve this problem, the zoos got together and created the Jaguar Species Survival Plan. The plan helps make sure jaguars in zoos have new mates who are not from their own families.

I am an important part of that plan because I am not related to any of the jaguars living in zoos. My genes are different from theirs. If I mate with another jaguar in the zoo, my genes will help the cubs be strong and healthy. My cubs can grow up and pass my genes on to their own healthy cubs. They will help make the population of jaguars living in zoos strong and healthy.

La gente estaba entusiasmada por mi llegada a Milwaukee. Para ellos yo significaba esperanza para el futuro de los jaguares. Es difícil para los jaguares en los zoológicos encontrar pareja porque muchos son de la misma familia. Si un macho y una hembra jaguar de la misma familia tienen cachorros juntos, sus crías pueden estar débiles y a menudo enfermizo. Para resolver este problema, los zoológicos se reunieron y crearon el Plan de Supervivencia de Especies de Jaguar. El plan asegura que los jaguares en los zoológicos tengan nuevas parejas que no sean de sus propias familias.

Soy parte importante del plan porque no soy familiar de ninguno de los jaguares que viven en los zoológicos. Mis genes son diferentes a los suyos. Si me apareo con otro jaguar en el zoológico, mis genes ayudarás a los cachorros a ser fuertes y sanos. Mis cachorros pueden crecer y así pasar mis genes a sus cachorros saludables. Ayudarán a que la población de jaguares viviendo en los zoológicos sea fuerte y saludable.

Species

A species is a group of living things that can reproduce its own kind. Jaguars are a species. Jaguars have jaguar cubs.

Especies

Una especie es un grupo de cosas vivientes que pueden reproducir su propia especie. Los jaguares son una especie. Los jaguares tienen cachorros jaguar.

Genetic diversity is important for the health of a species.

La diversidad genética es importante para la salud de las especies.

Genes

Genes are codes in the body that contain all the traits that are passed on to an animal from its parents.

Genes

Los genes son códigos en el cuerpo que contienen todos los rasgos que son transmitidos al animal por sus padres.

Humans are the only natural enemy of jaguars.

Los humanos son los únicos enemigos naturales de los jaguares.

However, when I first arrived in Wisconsin, I didn't know any of that. My first breath of Milwaukee air was a shock. Something almost painful hit my lungs. Cold air. My whole body shivered. My eyes began to water. How could the air be so cold that it hurt just to stand in it? It was a relief when I was loaded into the back of a warm truck.

The people drove me to the Animal Health Center at the Milwaukee County Zoo. Zoos have to follow a rule that new mammals must stay in quarantine, away from all other animals, for thirty days. The veterinarians at the center examined me and did tests to make sure I wasn't sick or didn't have a disease that might be dangerous to other animals. I had to stay in quarantine longer than normal because the veterinarians discovered I had parasites. They gave me medicine and took good care of me. While I was in quarantine, a dentist checked my teeth. He found that the dentist in Belize had done excellent work on my teeth.

Sin embargo, cuando llegué por primera vez a Wisconsin, no sabía nada de eso. Mi primera bocanada de aire de Milwaukee fue una conmoción. Algo casi doloroso golpeó mis pulmones. Aire frío. Todo mi cuerpo tembló. Mis ojos lagrimeaban. ¿Cómo podía ser tan frío el aire que dolía sólo estar ahí? Fue un alivio cuando me llevaron a la parte trasera de un camión con calefacción.

La gente me llevó al Centro de Salud Animal en el zoológico del condado de Milwaukee. Los zoológicos tienen que seguir una regla, que los mamíferos recién llegados tienen que estar en cuarentena, lejos de otros animales, por treinta días. Los veterinarios del Centro me examinaron y me hicieron análisis para asegurarse de que yo no estaba enfermo o que tuviera una enfermedad que pusiera en peligro a otros animales. Tuve que estar en cuarentena más tiempo que el normal porque los veterinarios descubrieron que tenía parásitos. Me dieron medicina y me cuidaron muy bien. Mientras estuve en cuarentena un dentista checó mis dientes. Encontró que el dentista en Belice había hecho un excelente trabajo con mis dientes.

In Belize even during the cooler, dry season, the temperature is usually between 60° F and 80° F (15° C and 27° C). On the day Pat arrived in Milwaukee it was a nearly freezing 34° F (1° C).

En Belice, inclusive durante el frío y la temporada seca, la temperatura generalmente es de entre 60º F y 80º F (15º C y 27º C). El día que Pat llegó a Milwaukee estaba casi congelado, había 34º F (1º C).

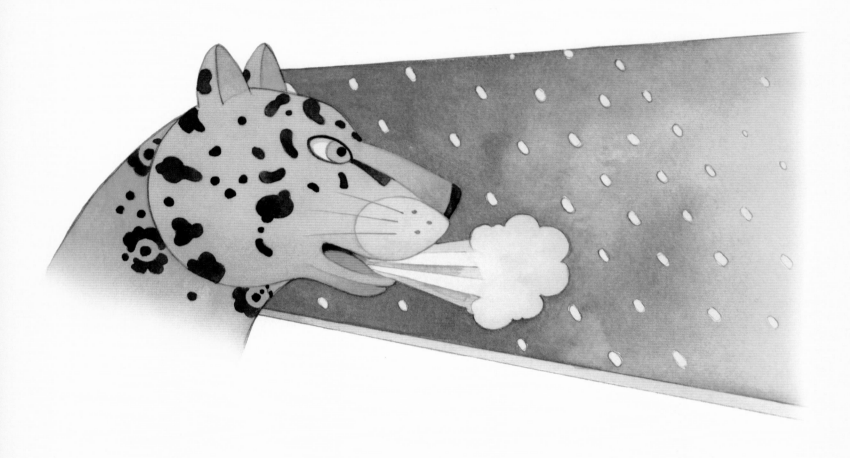

Quarantine

Quarantine means to put an animal in a place away from others in case the animal has a disease that could spread.

Cuarentena

La cuarentena significa poner a un animal en un lugar alejado de otros en caso de que el animal tenga una enfermedad que se pudiera contagiar.

Parasite

A parasite is an organism that survives by living on or in another animal and feeding on that animal.

Parásito

Un parásito es un organismo que sobrevive viviendo en otro animal y alimentándose de ese animal.

My caretaker was gentle and took very good care of me, but there was nobody familiar in the Animal Health Center, like Junior Buddy or the zoo lady with the red hair. Then one day the couple I knew from Belize came to see me. They talked to me and spent time with me. It felt good to know that even though I had come a long way, something was familiar that connected me to my home in Belize.

Mi cuidador era gentil y cuidó muy bien de mí, pero no había ningún familiar en el Centro de Salud Animal, como Junior Buddy o la señora pelirroja del zoológico. Entonces, un día, la pareja que conocí de Belice vinieron a verme. Me hablaron y pasaron tiempo conmigo. Se sentía bien saber que aunque había venido en un viaje largo, algo me era conocido y me conectaba a mi hogar en Belice.

Welcome to your new home Pat, where you are surrounded by love!

¡Bienvenido a tu nuevo hogar Pat, donde estás rodeado de amor!

Zoos are important because they teach people about animals. They help many animals that have lost their habitats.

Los zoológicos son importantes porque enseñan a l gente acerca de animales. Ayudan a muchos animales que han perdido sus hábitats.

CHAPTER 12

Pat in Big Cat Country

After quarantine, I was moved to my den in the part of the zoo called Big Cat Country. There are tree trunks, rocks, and logs for me to climb on. **Three kind zookeepers take care of me.** Every day one of them feeds me three pounds (1.4 kilograms) of a mix of ground beef, heart, liver, vitamins, and minerals. Once or twice a week, one of the zookeepers will toss me a big cow bone. It feels good to gnaw on the bones.

The place where I eat has a jumble of logs stacked all the way up to a very high ceiling. There is a window in the ceiling where the sun shines in. After chewing on a bone, I climb to the top of the logs and stretch out in the sunshine.

Pat en el País de los Grandes Gatos

Después de la cuarentena, Me llevaron a mi cueva en la parte del zoológico llamada País del Gran Gato. Ahí hay leños de árbol, rocas y troncos para que trepe en ellos. Me cuidan tres clases de cuidadores del zoológico. Cada día uno de ellos me alimentan con tres libras (1.4 kilos) de una mezcla de carne de res molida, corazón, hígado, vitaminas y minerales. Una o dos veces por semana, uno de los cuidadores me avienta un gran hueso de vaca. Se siente bien roer los huesos.

El lugar donde como tiene un lugar enorme de leños encimados hasta arriba de un techo muy alto. Hay una ventana en el techo donde brilla el sol. Después de estar masticando un hueso, subo a la cima de los leños y me estiro en el sol.

Now Pat lives in a safe place, and is taken care of by the people at the zoo.

Ahora Pat vive en un lugar seguro y es cuidado por la gente del zoológico.

Jaguars put smiles on children's faces.

Los jaguares ponen sonrisas en la caras de los niños.

People who don't know about jaguars can learn
how great they are when they are at the zoo.

La gente que no sabe acerca de los jaguares
puede aprender qué buenos son cuando
los observa en el zoológico.

Everyone was happy
to meet Pat the Cat!

¡Todos estuvieron contentos de
conocer a Pat the Cat, Pato el Gato!

When I first arrived in Big Cat Country, I could smell other animals, but I didn't know what they were. They didn't smell familiar and I couldn't see them. One day I roared and was answered by another animal with the loudest roar I had ever heard. I realized it must have come from a much bigger cat. I ducked low and slunk to the back of my den to hide.

Cuando llegué por primera vez al País de los Grandes Gatos (Big Cat Country), podía oler otros animales, pero no sabía que eran. No tenían un olor conocido y no los podía ver. Un día rugí y me contestó otro animal con el rugido más fuerte que hubiera yo oído. Pensé que debería de venir de un gato más grande. Me escabullí para esconderme al fondo de mi cueva.

The Zoo prepared for Pat by remodeling his private den, raising the ceiling panels, and adding logs for Pat to climb high up to reach the skylight. Outside, they added a log climbing structure so that Pat could watch all that went on around him, resting high upon logs, just as he had in Belize.

El zoológico se preparó para Pat remodelando su cueva privada, subiendo los paneles del techo y poniendo troncos para que Pat trepe para alcanzar la luz del cielo. Afuera, ellos pusieron una gran estructura, así que Pat podía trepar y observar todo lo que pasaba a su alrededor, descansando en lo alto de los leños, como acostumbraba hacerlo en Belice.

To be called a great cat, you have to be a cat that roars. There are four great cats: tigers, lions, leopards, and jaguars, but only the jaguar calls the Americas home.

Para que un felino sea llamado un gran gato tiene que ser un gato que ruge. Hay cuatro grandes gatos: tigres, leones, leopardos y jaguares, pero únicamente el jaguar es nativo de América.

The first neighbor I saw in Big Cat Country was **an enormous lion** with a great shaggy mane. Down the hall from the lion a tiger was lying on the floor of its den. At the time I didn't know "lion" or "tiger." All I knew was that just a few feet away from me were two very large cats. I had never seen anything like them before.

I ran to the back of my den, panting, baring my teeth, and growling. The zookeeper tried to soothe me. "You're okay, Pat. That's a good boy. They're not going to hurt you. Take it easy, boy."

Over time I began to relax. I decided the other cats were not coming to attack me. They didn't even seem to notice me much. Now I feel safe in Big Cat Country. The zookeepers gave me a big ball to play with. I can jump and scratch, nap and play in my den.

El primer vecino que vi en el País de los Grandes Gatos (Big Cat Country) fue un enorme león con una gran melena enmarañada. Más allá del corredor del león un tigre estaba echado en el suelo de su cueva. En ese entonces no sabía que era "león" o "tigre". Lo único que sabía es que no muy lejos de mi estaban dos grandes gatos. Nunca antes había visto algo como ellos.

Corrí al fondo de mi cueva, jadeando, mostrando mis dientes y gruñendo. El cuidador del zoológico trató de calmarme. "Estás bien Pat. Eres un buen niño. No te van a hacer daño. Tómalo con calma, muchacho."

Con el tiempo empecé a relajarme. Decidí que los otros gatos no querían venir a atacarme. Parecía que ni siquiera me prestaban atención. Ahora me siento seguro en el País de los Grandes Gatos (Big Cat Country). Los cuidadores me dieron una gran pelota para jugar. Puedo brincar, rasguñar, dormir la siesta y jugar en mi cueva.

The jaguar is the third largest feline in the world.
Only the tiger and the lion are bigger.

El jaguar es el tercer felino más grande del mundo.
Sólo el tigre y el león son más grandes.

Lions and tigers do not live
in the wild in the Americas.

Los leones y tigres no viven
en estado salvaje en América.

CHAPTER 13

Pat's Joyful Roar

Sometime later the zookeepers introduced me to my outdoor yard for the first time. It had been a very long time since I had been outside. When they opened the door, I bounded out into the sunlight and filled my lungs with the fresh, clean, fall air. I lifted my head to the breeze and scanned the sky with my eyes. Birds were flying overhead. The breeze carried with it the familiar scent of tapirs from the forest of Belize. How could that be? Then I could see them right there below me: tapirs!

Crouching, I began slowly stalking the tapirs. It felt good to be stalking again. The great hunter of the rainforest hadn't stalked anything for so long. As I approached, I saw a cliff separating me from the tapirs below. I'd never be able to jump across the wide gap to attack one, but it still felt good to stalk them. Then I noticed that beyond the tapirs was a railing. On the other side of the railing stood many of my friends smiling and watching me: the zookeepers, the people in charge of the animals, and the couple who had helped me in Belize.

El feliz rugido de Pat

Algún tiempo después los cuidadores del zoológico me llevaron al patio exterior por primera vez. Había pasado mucho tiempo desde que la última vez que había estado al aire libre. Cuando abrieron la puerta, salí a la luz del día y llené mis pulmones con aire otoñal fresco y limpio. Levanté mi cabeza a la brisa y miré el cielo. Había pájaros volando arriba. La brisa traía el familiar olor de los tapires de la selva tropical de Belice. ¿Cómo podía ser? Lo podía ver ahí mismo, debajo de mí: ¡tapires!

Agachándome empecé despacio a acechar a los tapires. Se sentía bien estar acechando otra vez. El gran cazador de la selva no había acechado nada por mucho tiempo. Mientras me acercaba, vi un acantilado separándome de los tapires de abajo. Nunca fui capaz de saltar la gran brecha para atacar a uno, pero aún así se sentía bien acecharlos. Entonces noté que más allá de los tapires había un cerco. Del otro lado del cerco había muchos de mis amigos sonriendo y mirándome: los cuidadores del zoológico, la gente encargada de los animales y la pareja que me había ayudado en Belice.

Pat's outdoor area is open all the way up
to the sky. There is a pond in his large yard.

El área exterior de Pat está abierta, todo el camino
hasta el cielo. Hay un estanque en su gran jardín.

People have to
respect the jaguar.

La gente tiene que
respetar a los jaguares.

89

I turned from the tapirs and the people. I ran to the jumbled pile of logs in my yard. I climbed up and leapt to the top of the highest log. There I stood, lifting my face to the sun. I let out my loudest roar. It was good to be a jaguar. **It was good to be alive.**

Dejé de ver a los tapires y a la gente. Corrí a la pila enorme de leños en mi jardín. Trepé y me lancé al leño más alto. Ahí estuve, levantando mi cara al sol. Dejé salir mi más ruidoso rugido. Era bueno ser un jaguar. Era bueno estar vivo.

Long live the jaguars!

¡Larga vida a los jaguares!

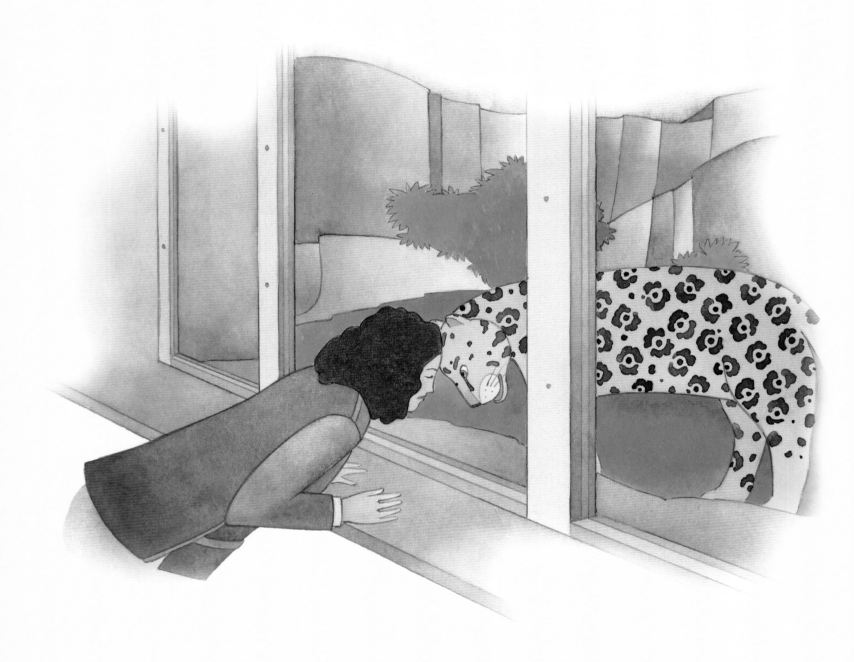

We should protect the jaguars so that
when we grow up, we will be able to
show them to our children.

Debemos proteger a los jaguares para que cuando
crezcamos podamos mostrárselos a nuestros hijos.

The people of Milwaukee are lucky to
have Pat living in their zoo.

La gente de Milwaukee es afortunada de tener
viviendo en su zoológico a Pat.

On another afternoon, I was stretched out on a rock in my yard, lazily watching the tapirs and the people below. People were looking at me from the glass sides of my yard, too. Then I saw a woman with curly, red hair approach the glass. I lifted my head. Something about her looked familiar. I stood and stretched. I yawned. I looked at her more closely. Could it be?

Yes, it could be. It really could be. I raced to the window, and before I got there, I caught her scent. I was sure. It was my old friend, the red-headed zoo lady from Belize! I ran straight for her. She pressed her forehead on the outside of the glass, and I pressed my forehead on my side. It was good to see my friend again.

Otra tarde estaba estirándome en una roca en mi jardín, observando perezosamente a los tapires y la gente de abajo. La gente me miraba también a través de los cristales laterales de mi jardín. Entonces vi a una mujer pelirroja con cabello rizado aproximándose al cristal. Levanté la cabeza. Algo en ella me resultaba familiar. Me levanté y estiré. Bostecé. La miré más de cerca. ¿Podía ser?

Sí, podía ser. De verdad podía ser. Corrí a la ventana y antes de llegar me llegó su aroma. Estaba seguro. Era mi vieja amiga, ¡la señora pelirroja del zoológico de Belice! Corrí directo hacia ella. Ella apoyaba su frente en el cristal exterior y yo apoyaba mi frente en mi lado. Era bueno ver a mi amiga otra vez.

CHAPTER 14

Pat the Ambassador

School children, families, and adults have come to see me again and again in my new home. They look into my shining eyes. They love my sleek golden fur with its beautiful rosette markings. People comment on the white fur under my chin and on my stomach. They like to see me flick my tail, tipped with black and gold rings. They see how powerful I am with my thick neck and muscled shoulders. It is something special when you can see a jaguar up close.

El Embajador Pat

Estudiantes, familias, y adultos han venido para verme una y otra vez en mi nuevo hogar. Ellos ven mis ojos brillantes. Les encanta mi pelo dorado con hermosas rosetas negras. La gente comenta de mi pelaje debajo de mi barbilla y en mi estómago. Les gusta verme mover la cola con anillos negros y dorados en la punta. Ven lo poderoso que soy con mi cuello grueso y hombros musculosos. Es algo especial cuando puedes ver a un jaguar de cerca.

Pat the Cat became the Ambassador of Belize!

¡Pat the Cat, Pat el Gato, se convirtió en el Embajador de Belice!

Ambassador
An ambassador is an official representative or messenger.

Embajador
Un embajador es un representante oficial o mensajero.

When a jaguar is fully grown, it is from four feet to six feet long, not counting the tail. Jaguars are about three feet tall from the ground to their shoulder when standing on all four paws. They usually weigh 100 to 250 pounds (45 to 115 kilograms).

Cuando un jaguar está completamente desarrollado, mide de cuatro a seis pies, sin contar la cola. La altura de los jaguares es cercana a los tres pies, cuando están parados en sus cuatro patas. Generalmente pesan de 100 a 250 libras (45 a 115 kilos).

Scientists are studying jaguars and their environments to learn more about them. They still have a lot to learn. Jaguars are hard to study because they live alone in the wild, avoiding people.

Los científicos están estudiando a los jaguares en su ambiente para aprender más de ellos. Todavía tienen mucho que aprender. Los jaguares son difíciles de estudiar porque viven solos en la naturaleza salvaje, evitando a la gente.

People almost never see jaguars in the wild.

La gente casi nunca ve jaguares en la naturaleza salvaje.

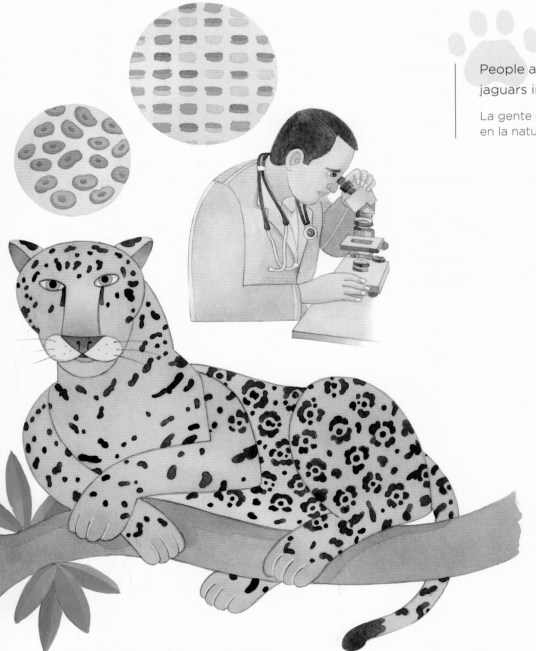

As a member of a keystone species, I am helping people learn about jaguars and understand our importance in the ecosystem. Because jaguars are at the top of the food chain, the health of our ecosystem depends upon us. If jaguars, the top predators, are healthy, then other animals and even plants in the ecosystem may live in balance as well. Today, fewer jaguars than ever roam the wild because we are losing our habitats and our prey. If jaguars are in trouble, so are our ecosystems.

Como miembro de una especie clave, estoy ayudando a la gente aprender acerca de los jaguares y a entender nuestra importancia en el ecosistema. Porque los jaguares están en la cima de la cadena alimenticia, la salud de nuestro ecosistema depende de nosotros. Si los jaguares, los principales depredadores, somos saludables, entonces otros animales e incluso plantas del ecosistema pueden vivir en equilibrio también. Hoy menos jaguares que nunca deambulan por la naturaleza salvaje, estamos perdiendo nuestros hábitats y nuestras presas. Si los jaguares están en problemas, también lo está nuestro ecosistema.

Keystone Species

A keystone species is a very important animal in its ecosystem. The health of the keystone species affects the health of all the other animals in their ecosystem.

Especies clave

Las especies clave son animales muy importantes en su ecosistema. La salud del animal clave de las especies afecta la salud de todos los otros animales pertenecientes a su ecosistema.

In the 1960's as many as 18,000 jaguars were killed every year for their fur coats. Now it's illegal to hunt jaguars, but some people still hunt jaguars for their skins.

En la década de los sesentas, mataron cada año a 18,000 jaguares para tener su piel. Ahora es ilegal cazar jaguares, pero algunos todavía cazan jaguares por su piel.

Humans are the only natural enemy of jaguars.

Los humanos son los únicos enemigos naturales de los jaguares.

Ecosystem

An ecosystem is an environment that has all kinds of living and non-living things.

Ecosistema

Un ecosistema es un ambiente que tiene toda clase de cosas vivas y sin vida.

It is said that I am an ambassador for my species. This means that I represent my species to the world. This is one big job. So the children in Milwaukee, Wisconsin, USA, and in Belize, Central America, have come together to help create this book. They worked hard! And they inspired many other children across nations to join in.

Kids are creative! They are writing stories, poems, and songs. They are drawing pictures, making jaguar masks, and even writing a comic book about saving jaguars. I am very grateful, because if we jaguars are to survive, we are going to need a lot of ambassadors who will speak for us.

Se dice que soy un embajador de mi especie. Esto significa que represento a mi especie en el mundo. Este es un gran trabajo. Así que los niños en Milwaukee, Wisconsin, EU, y en Belice, Centroamérica, se han unido para ayudar a crear este libro. ¡Han trabajado duro! Y han inspirado a muchos otros niños a unirse alrededor de otras naciones.

¡Los niños son creativos! Están escribiendo cuentos, poemas, y canciones. Están dibujando retratos, haciendo máscaras de jaguar, inclusive escribiendo una historieta cómica acerca de salvar jaguares. Estoy muy agradecido porque si nosotros los jaguares vamos a sobrevivir, vamos a necesitar a muchos embajadores que hablen por nosotros.

According to the Endangered Species Act, jaguars are endangered. They are listed as near threatened by the International Union for Conservation of Nature.

De acuerdo con la Ley de Especies en Peligro de Extinción, los jaguares están en peligro. Son considerados una especie amenazada por la Unión Internacional para la Conservación de la Naturaleza.

Jaguars keep their ecosystem in balance. Without jaguars, the other animals in their habitats would become overpopulated. There would not be enough food for all of them.

Los jaguares mantienen su ecosistema en equilibrio. Sin los jaguares, el hábitat de otros animales estaría sobrepoblado. No habría suficiente comida para todos ellos.

CHAPTER 15

Pat and Stella

Lately I have been making friends with **a female jaguar named Stella.** She is shy around me, but I am very patient and gentle with her.

The first time the zookeepers let Stella into my den, I was stretched out on a log high up near the ceiling. She walked all around the inside of my space, careful to avoid me. I kept very still. Stella made several visits like this. She would not come near me, and I grew impatient. One day I finally approached Stella. I tried to snuggle my face against hers. She reared back on her hind legs and batted my head with her front paws. Thankfully, she had kept her claws retracted so she didn't cut me, but I got the message loud and clear. Stella was not ready to be close to me. I will have to be patient.

Pat y Stella

Últimamente he estado haciendo amistad con una hembra jaguar llamada Stella. Es tímida a mí alrededor, pero yo soy muy paciente y gentil con ella.

La primera vez que los cuidadores del zoológico dejaron a Stella en mi cueva, estaba echado en un tronco alto casi cerca del techo. Ella caminó alrededor del interior de mi espacio, con cuidado para evitarme. Me mantuve muy quieto. Stella hizo varias visitas como esta. No se acercaba a mí, y empecé a impacientarme. Un día por fin me acerqué a Stella. Traté de frotar mi cara contra la suya. Ella se movió hacia atrás en sus patas traseras y golpeó mi cabeza con su pata delantera. Por suerte había mantenido guardadas sus garras para no cortarme, pero entendí el mensaje fuerte y claramente. Stella no estaba lista para estar cerca de mí. Tendré que ser paciente.

Jaguars have large paws with sharp claws. They keep their claws retracted, or pulled in, when they are not using them for fighting, climbing, scratching, or hunting.

Los jaguares tienen grandes patas de afiladas garras. Mantienen sus garras retraídas o hacia adentro cuando no las están usando para pelear, trepar, rasguñar o cazar.

If Stella and I have cubs together, our cubs will be special and important because I am not related to any of the other jaguars in captivity. Our cubs will grow up and have strong, healthy cubs with jaguars from other zoos. Because of Stella and me, future generations of jaguars in zoos may be healthy and strong.

Si Stella y yo tenemos cachorros, nuestros cachorros serán especiales e importantes porque no tengo parentesco alguno con ninguno de los otros jaguares en cautiverio. Nuestros cachorros crecerán y tendrán cachorros fuertes y saludables con jaguares de otros zoológicos. Stella y yo seremos responsables de que las futuras generaciones de jaguares en zoológicos sean saludables y fuertes.

I even met a girl cat named Stella
They tell me she's my mate,
We are getting to know each other first
Cubs will have to wait!

Incluso conocí a una jaguar llamada Stella.
Me dicen que es mi compañera,
Estamos llegando a conocernos primero
¡Los cachorros tendrán que esperar!

CHAPTER 16

Pat's Dream

One afternoon, not long ago, I was stretched out on the highest log in my outdoor yard, in the warm sunshine. I looked at my pond, my trees, and the puffy white clouds floating high in the blue sky. The tapirs were grazing lazily in the yard below, and people had gathered along the railing. This wasn't Belize. It wasn't the rainforest, but I knew with my damaged leg and teeth that I would never be able to go home to stalk prey in the wild again.

I rested my jaw on one massive paw and drifted off to sleep. **I began to dream.** I felt my body rise, up and up. I rose up over the trees in my yard, so high I could see all of Big Cat Country. Looking down as I dreamed, I saw Stella some day in the future, wrestling playfully with a fuzzy, grey-furred cub. It was my cub.

In my dream I drifted higher in the warm sunshine, so high I could see jaguars being well cared for in many other zoos.

El sueño de Pat

Una tarde, no hace mucho tiempo, estaba echado en el tronco más alto de mi jardín exterior, bajo el cálido sol. Miré mi estanque, mis árboles y las pomposas nubes blancas flotando en el cielo azul. Los tapires estaban pastoreando tranquilamente en el patio de abajo, y la gente se reunía a lo largo de la valla. Esto no era Belice. No era la selva tropical, pero sabía que con mi pata y con mis dientes dañados no podría nunca regresar a casa para acechar presas en la naturaleza salvaje.

Apoyé la mandíbula en mi pata imponente lentamente me dormí. Empecé a soñar. Sentí mi cuerpo elevarse. Me elevé arriba de los arboles en mi jardín, tan alto que podía ver todo el País de los Grandes Gatos (Big Cat Country). Mirando hacia abajo mientras soñaba, vi cómo sería Stella algún día en el futuro, luchando juguetonamente con un cachorro con pelusa gris. Era mi cría.

En mi sueño me elevaba en el cálido sol, tan alto que podía ver a los jaguares bien cuidados en muchos otros zoológicos.

I have a friend who lost her home, too. It was sad for my friend, and it was sad that Pat lost his home. After a while my friend found a new home, and she was happy. Now Pat the Cat has found a home at the Milwaukee County Zoo. I think Pat must be happy.

Tengo una amiga que también perdió su casa. Fue triste para mi amiga, y fue triste para Pat perder su casa. Después de un tiempo, mi amiga encontró una nueva casa y fue feliz. Ahora Pat el gato ha encontrado su hogar en el zoológico del Condado de Milwaukee. Pienso que Pat debe de estar contento.

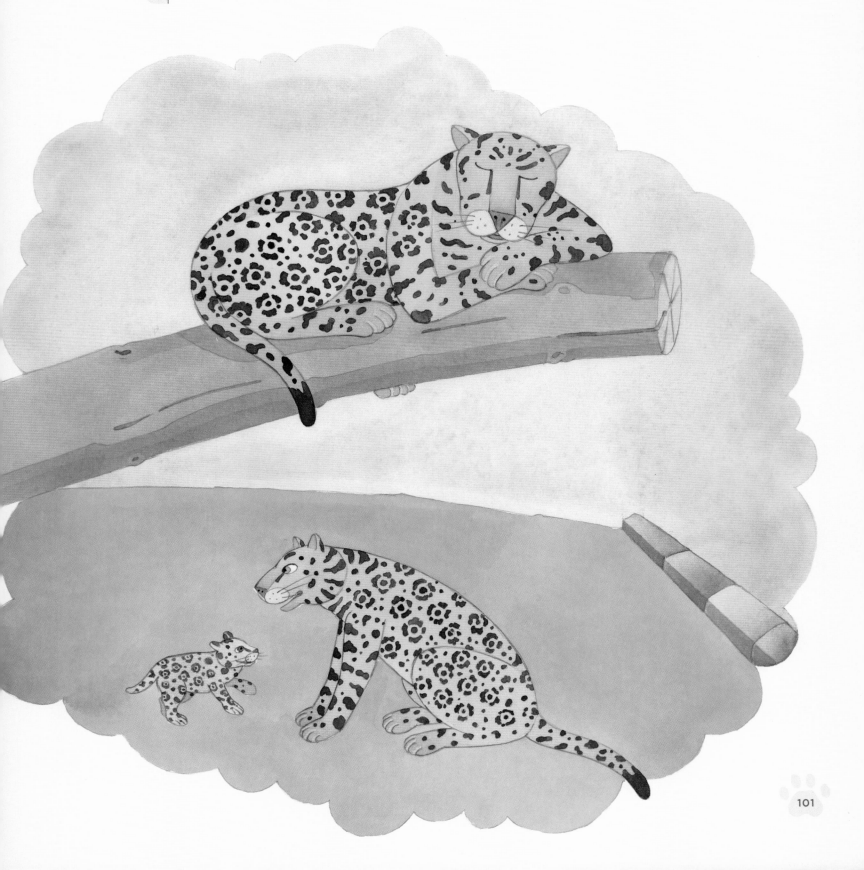

I soared higher in my dream. I sped through the clouds until the trees and the land below changed. I was flying over Central and South America.

I saw the jaguar preserve of Belize. I saw the jaguar corridors created by Belize, other governments in the Americas, and Panthera. The corridors were like beautiful green lace stretching from Mexico to the tip of Argentina. The corridors were safe passages for jaguars to travel to find prey, mates, and new territories.

In my wonderful dream, I drifted closer to the earth. I could see the beautiful country of Belize, then Belize City, and finally the Belize Zoo. There the zookeepers were taking care of jaguars in the rehabilitation program.

Me elevaba más en mi sueño. Corrí velozmente a través de las nubes hasta que abajo cambiaban los árboles y la tierra. Estaba volando sobre Centro y Sudamérica.

Vi protegido al jaguar de Belice. Vi los corredores del jaguar creados por Belice, otros gobiernos de las Américas y Panthera. Los corredores eran como un hermoso encaje verde extendiéndose de México hasta la punta de Argentina. Los corredores eran parajes seguros para que los jaguares recorrieran para encontrar presas, parejas y nuevos territorios.

En mi sueño maravilloso volaba cerca de la tierra. Podía ver el hermoso país de Belice, luego la ciudad de Belice y finalmente el zoológico de Belice. Ahí los cuidadores del zoológico estaban cuidando a los jaguares en el programa de rehabilitación.

I am happy for Pat, but his story makes me worry about what is happening to other jaguars in the wild.

Estoy feliz por Pat, pero su historia hace que me preocupe acerca de lo que está pasando con otros jaguares en estado salvaje.

If people work together, these beautiful spotted cats will roam the wild lands of the Americas for years to come.

Si la gente trabaja junta, estos hermosos gatos de negro pelaje y doradas rosetas recorrerán las tierras salvajes de las Américas en los años venideros.

Jaguar Corridors
- Jaguar Corridors
- Jaguar Populations

My country established the very first jaguar preserve in the world. We are happy that we are protecting the jaguars, and their home, the rainforest. So let us all protect the great cat of the Americas!

Mi país estableció la primera reserva del jaguar en el mundo. Estamos felices que estamos protegiendo al jaguar y a su casa, la selva. Así que protejamos todos al ¡Gran Gato de las Américas!

This is the message children can pass on
to future generations: Save the jaguars!

Este es el mensaje que los niños pueden dar a las
futuras generaciones: ¡Salven a los jaguares!

I am sure glad that so many people shared their compassion and
empathy with Pat, or else he may not be around today. It would be a
shame destroying something so valuable and wild and yet so vulnerable.

De seguro estoy contento que mucha gente comparta su compasión y
empatía con Pat o de lo contrario no estaría hoy aquí. Sería una lástima
destruir algo tan valioso y salvaje y, sin embargo, tan vulnerable.

It's up to us to protect the jaguar —
the big cat of the Americas!

Está en nosotros proteger al jaguar —
¡el Gran Gato de las Américas!

Then I saw the **children throughout the Americas working together** to tell the world about the beauty of jaguars. They were teaching the people about the need to protect our place in the world.

I floated onward in my dream, over the emerald green rainforests near Honey Camp Lagoon. Then my breath caught in my throat. From high in the sky, I saw the waterfall I had known so well as a cub. It was my mother's territory, and there stretched out on the high rock above the falls, shining in the sun, was a glorious black jaguar. It was my very own sister, caressing her cubs, one black like herself and one golden like me. They were my own family, living on in the wild.

Finally I understood why I had to leave my beautiful forest home and fly alone to a new life in Milwaukee. I needed to help all jaguars, captive and free.

I am the voice of the jaguars, calling people everywhere to save us and preserve our wild habitats. With all my heart, I hope the people will share my dream.

Together we can save the jaguars.

Entonces vi a los niños a lo largo de las Américas trabajando juntos para decirle al mundo acerca de la belleza de los jaguares. Estaban enseñando a la gente acerca de la necesidad de proteger nuestro lugar en el mundo.

En mi sueño flotaba hacia adelante, sobre la selva verde esmeralda cerca de Honey Campo Lagoon. Entonces me quedé sin aire. Desde lo alto en el cielo vi la cascada que tan bien conocí cuando yo era tan sólo un cachorro. Era el territorio de mi madre, se extendía a la roca más alta por arriba de la cascada, brillando en el sol estaba un glorioso jaguar negro. Era mi propia hermana, cuidando a sus cachorros, uno negro como ella y otro dorado como yo. Eran mi propia familia, viviendo en la naturaleza salvaje.

Finalmente entendí por qué tuve que abandonar mi hermoso hogar del bosque y volar solo a una nueva vida en Milwaukee. Necesitaba ayudar a todos los jaguares, a los cautivos y a los libres.

Soy la voz de los jaguares llamando a la gente de todas partes para salvarnos y proteger nuestro hábitat silvestre. Con todo mi corazón, tengo la esperanza de que la gente comparta mi sueño.

Juntos podemos salvar a los jaguares.

Remember: The jaguar is our big cat!

Recuerden: ¡El jaguar es nuestro gran gato!

MAP OF THE AMERICAS

The Americas include North, Central, and South America.

Today there are many people from all over the world living in both Belize and the United States. There are all kinds of people living, working, and playing together. We call that diversity.

Canada

Milwaukee

U.S.A.

NORTH AMERICA

Belize

CENTRAL AMERICA

SOUTH AMERICA

Minnesota

Lake *Superior*

Michigan Upper Peninsula

Wisconsin

Iowa

Milwaukee

Lake Michigan

Illinois

Wisconsin is bordered on the west by the state of Minnesota, the south by the state of Illinois, the north by Lake Superior and Michigan's Upper Peninsula, and the east by Lake Michigan.

In 1848 Wisconsin was admitted to the United States as the 30th state.

About 46% of Wisconsin is covered by temperate forests.

Wisconsin covers 54,310 square miles (140,662 square kilometers). It is about six times larger than Belize.

English is the official language of Belize. Many people in Belize also speak Spanish. There are other languages spoken in Belize, including Kriol, Garifuna, and some that originated with the Maya people.

Belize is bordered on the west by Mexico and Guatemala and on the east by the Caribbean Sea.

Belize was part of Great Britain from 1840 until it gained its independence in 1981. It was known as British Honduras until 1973 when its name was changed to Belize.

Over half of Belize is covered with tropical rainforests.

Mexico

Honey Camp Lagoon

Guatemala

Belize Zoo
X

Belize

Caribbean Sea

Belize is 176 miles (283 kilometers) long and 88 miles (142 kilometers) wide. It has almost 200 islands. It has 8,867 square miles (22,965 square kilometers) of land.

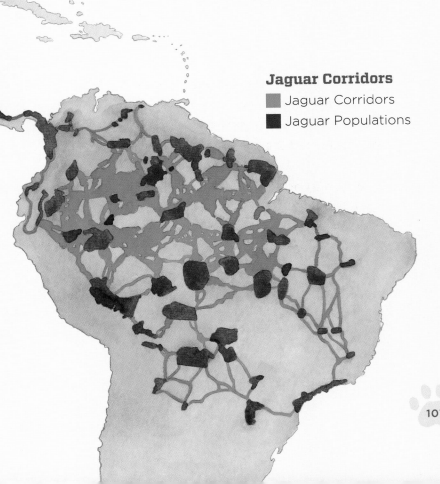

Jaguar Corridors
- Jaguar Corridors
- Jaguar Populations

Wisconsin has four seasons: winter, spring, summer, and fall. Belize has two seasons: wet and dry.

The average temperature in Wisconsin in January is between 11 and 26° F (-12 and -3° C). The average temperature in Belize in January is 70 to 80° F (21 to 27° C).

The southern part of Wisconsin receives an average of 50 inches (127 cm) of snow each winter. It never snows in Belize. Belize receives up to 160 inches (407 cm) of rainfall in a year, but Wisconsin receives only about 35 inches (89 cm) of rainfall in a year.

The rainforest canopy is formed by trees that are 65 to 130 feet (20 to 40 meters) tall. Canopy trees receive plenty of sunlight to convert into energy. They produce a wealth of food for birds, bats, insects, frogs, and lizards.

Once upon a time there was a jaguar that lived in the rainforest of Belize. His home was chopped down and ranchers moved in. He didn't know what to do. He couldn't live in his home anymore and he had nowhere to go. Then some people helped him find a home at the Milwaukee County Zoo in Wisconsin, U.S.A. Do you like my story? Guess what? It's true! There really is a jaguar from Belize that had to leave his rainforest home and now lives at the Milwaukee County Zoo. His name is Pat the Cat. You should go see him! If you go, tell him we said, "Hello!"

I hope the animals are respected as part of our diversity.

Imagine someone took down your walls, roof, and removed your furniture. It wouldn't really feel like your home, but rather like you had been kicked out.

Pat the Cat is a jaguar from Belize that had to go to the Milwaukee County Zoo because he was in danger. There aren't many jaguars left. That is why Pat had to be saved. Now Pat is safe, and we know the jaguars won't be extinct.

What was I left to do? Hungry, homeless, helpless. Then I saw them. You humans call them steak, hamburger, ribs. I too decided to call them dinner. Well, as you can guess, the farmer who paid big money for his cattle was a bit upset with me. What they considered murder, I still call dinner.

The jaguar has an excellent sense of hearing and vision. The jaguar hunts mostly at dawn and dusk, and his senses help him find prey. Jaguars can retract their claws.

Rainforests once covered 14% of the earth's land surface. Now they cover only 6% of the surface.

If you are in Milwaukee in January, you have to wear a coat, hat, gloves, boots, thick socks, and a scarf. In Belize you could wear flip flops, a t-shirt, and shorts.

Here's a weather fact that is also a math fact! Some parts of the world use Fahrenheit degrees to tell how hot or cold it is, and some use Celsius degrees. So, knowing how to convert temperature from one to the other can be a very useful skill!

To convert a Fahrenheit temperature to Celsius, subtract 32 from your Fahrenheit number, multiply this number by 5, and divide by 9 to get your Celsius temperature!

To convert a Celsius temperature to Fahrenheit, multiply your Celsius number by 9, divide this number by 5, and add 32 to this number to get your Fahrenheit temperature!

Now you're ready to travel (and you'll know the right clothes to bring)!

• WISDOM • JUSTICE • COURAGE • COMPASSION • HOPE • RESPECT •

Do Unto Others

Do unto others as you want them to do unto you.

Would you like your home to be destroyed?
Would you like your food to be taken away?
Would you like to live in fear?

Do unto others as you want them to do unto you!

Would you like it if you were helped when you struggled?
Would you like it if you were taught when you did wrong?
Would you like it if you were protected and helped along?

Do unto others as you want them to do unto you!

The jaguar is an animal,
A living creature,
The great American cat.

Do unto the jaguar as you want others to do unto you!

Pat had to get used to living in a closed in area. He needed to get acquainted with human contact. He also needed to get used to having other animals in close quarters to him especially other jaguars. He also had to get used to the smells of other large cats.

Jaguars
Are endangered because people are destroying their habitat
Great hunters, gorgeous, graceful
Use keen instincts to survive
Athletic, able to hunt
Radiant, robust, and rare
Sleek, speedy, strong, shrinking habitat...

Meet the jaguars, the biggest cats in the Americas.
Enjoy them for their beauty. Don't let them become extinct.
We need them to be here on earth for a long, long time.

The jungle (tropical rain forest) of Belize has animals, trees, and plants. The word jungle comes from the Sanskrit word *jangala*. The jungle of Belize is disappearing because the people are disturbing the animals' and plants' homes. People use wood to build houses, tables, and more. If the forests disappear, animals will be extinct, and all of these beautiful animals will disappear.

Here's a measurement fact that is also a math fact! Some parts of the world use inches as a unit of measurement, and some use centimeters. A centimeter, a metric measurement, is smaller than an inch.

Here's how to convert one to the other:
Inches to centimeters: Multiply the number of inches by 2.54 to get the measurement in centimeters.
Centimeters to inches: Multiply the number of centimeters by 0.394 to get the measurement in inches.

Among the Maya people, the jaguar symbolized "power and strength." It is seen on pottery and glyphs, and warriors also dressed as jaguars. It was believed that a jaguar could communicate between the dead and the living.

The Maya thought the jaguar was the most important animal of all. They believed that jaguars were gods. They believed the spots on their fur represented the stars, sun, and moon, and that jaguars had power because they were at the top of the food chain.

About three miles from Orange Walk where Pat once lived was one of the earliest Maya settlements. The Mayas made products out of obsidian like tools and weapons. They used jade for statues and jewelry, animal skins for clothing, bird feathers, honey dried fish, cotton and cacao. Some Mayas were farmers and grew crops.

Sun flecks the ground through the canopy,
Paw prints and red spots from killing a deer.
There are always echoes in the night
That magic coat hiding the creature from us.
There are high tree branches where monkeys are swinging
From tree to tree.
That feeling of animal being watched
He is closer than you think.
Are you scared?
He is watching and waiting.

Our first step was to show Pat that he was loved so he could begin to trust us. We sang to him songs we thought cats might like. We continued to talk softly and sweetly to Pat along with many compliments. It never hurts to hear about what a pretty coat you have. When you're feeling down, it's always nice to have a friend come along and put an arm around you.

Zoos help animals like Pat have a good home.

COMPREHENSION QUESTIONS

CHAPTER 1: PAT THE CUB

1. How many cubs do jaguar mothers usually have?
2. Where did Pat live?
3. Why did Pat leave his den?
4. List four facts from this chapter about jaguars.
5. Identify Belize on the map on page 106. Locate these important lines of latitude: the Equator, the Tropic of Cancer, the Tropic of Capricorn.
6. Explain why Pat thought he would be able to get his own food.
7. Which would you choose, to go out hunting with Pat or to stay in the den with his sister? Explain why.
8. From what point of view is the story being told? Whose point of view is it?
9. From what point of view is the information given in the fact boxes?
10. Which part of this chapter do you think is the most interesting?
11. How might the chapter have ended differently if Pat's mother had not killed the snake?

CHAPTER 2: PAT THE HUNTER

1. What are the differences between jaguars and leopards?
2. How did Pat change as he grew?
3. Describe Pat when he was a small cub. Describe Pat when he was older.
4. What does it mean to "stay upwind"?
5. What is the relationship between Pat growing older and Pat hunting the peccaries?
6. Write a new title for this chapter.
7. Which is more important, for the peccary to live or for Pat to have food for his family? Why?

CHAPTER 3: PAT'S BEAUTIFUL HOME

1. What are the four levels of the rainforest?
2. Why is the toucan special in Belize?
3. What is a coati?
4. Explain what is meant by "I carried a map in my head."
5. What might have happened if Pat had been hungry when the coati family came to drink?
6. How might life have been different for Pat's mother and sister after he left them?
7. Describe the scene at the waterfall from the point of view of the coati mother.
8. Which would have been better, for Pat to go off on his own, or for Pat to stay with his family? Why?

CHAPTER 4: PAT ON HIS OWN

1. How many kinds of animals do jaguars eat?
2. Describe how Pat knew he had found the territory of another jaguar.
3. What happened when Pat found another jaguar?
4. Why did Pat think he could take care of himself?
5. What is deforestation?
6. Explain how people are using the natural resources of the rainforest.
7. Explain ways people are changing the environment.
8. Would you have run away from the big jaguar like Pat did? Why or why not?
9. Jaguars need the forest to live. People sometimes need to cut down the forest so they can have homes and food. Explain your plan for using the rainforest in a way that will meet the needs of both jaguars and people.
10. How would you feel if you were the other jaguar and Pat came into your territory?
11. Do you think it is a good thing or a bad thing for people to use the forest to make a life for their families? Explain your answer.

CHAPTER 5: PAT CLAIMS HIS TERRITORY

1. What is a habitat?
2. What are the different kinds of habitats jaguars can live in?
3. When was the Maya culture the leading society in Belize?
4. Describe contributions made by the Maya culture.
5. List three things the Maya believed about jaguars.
6. Describe Pat's new territory.
7. What do you expect Pat's life will be like in his new territory?
8. How is Pat's territory the same as his mother's territory? How is it different?
9. What do you think about Pat living alone in his own territory?

CHAPTER 6: PAT IS INJURED

1. What does solitary mean?
2. Why doesn't Pat see many tapirs in the forest?
3. Why is it very dangerous for an animal in the wild to become injured?
4. What are the two seasons in Belize?
5. Describe in detail how Pat was injured and how his injury affects him. Use details from the story in your description.
6. What do you think will happen to Pat next?
7. If you were alone and became injured, what would you do?

8. Describe the factual information shown in the table about the seasons in Belize. Explain how this information adds to the story.

9. If Pat had not fallen, how might the chapter have ended differently?

10. How would you feel if you were Pat in this chapter?

CHAPTER 7: PAT DISCOVERS CATTLE

1. Why was Pat constantly hungry?

2. What were the changes Pat found in his territory?

3. Why was Pat able to capture the cow?

4. Who do you think owns the cattle?

5. What does this sentence mean: "Finally my hunger pushed me onward."?

6. Tell what you think would have happened if people saw Pat with the cattle.

7. Would you attack the cattle if you were Pat? Why or why not?

8. How would you solve Pat's problem of being unable to catch wild prey?

9. Do you think it was right or wrong for Pat to attack the cattle? Explain your answer.

CHAPTER 8: PAT IS CAPTURED

1. What happened the day after Pat ate the cow?

2. Why did Pat go back to the ranch?

3. Who is trying to teach people to manage their ranches without killing jaguars?

4. Describe in your own words how Pat was captured.

5. What would you do if an animal was taking food from your family?

6. How might the chapter have been different if Pat was not captured?

7. Why do you think the people trapped Pat in the cage?

8. Think of a solution to the problem of people needing to keep their cattle alive and jaguars needing food to eat.

9. Rewrite part of this chapter from the point of view of the people. Explain how their point of view changes how the events are described.

10. Do you think the people should have trapped Pat? Why or why not?

CHAPTER 9: PAT GETS HELP

1. Where did the people first take Pat for help?

2. Why could Pat no longer survive in the wild?

3. Where did the people from the Belize Forest Department take Pat?

4. What is the country of Belize doing to help jaguars?

5. What is Panthera's plan to help jaguars?

6. What is the biggest threat to jaguars?

7. Give four examples of places where jaguars no longer live.

8. Explain why jaguars need to be able to travel long distances.

9. Explain how corridors will help jaguars.

10. What is the relationship between jaguars and human activity in jaguar habitats?

11. Why do you think the people helped Pat instead of killing him?

CHAPTER 10: PAT AT THE BELIZE ZOO

1. How does the Problem Jaguar Rehabilitation Program help jaguars?

2. Describe the things Pat had to get used to at the Belize Zoo.

3. Describe the relationship between Pat and Junior Buddy.

4. What are the differences between Pat's life in the wild and Pat's life at the zoo?

5. Compare and contrast the lives of Pat and Junior Buddy. How are they the same? How are they different?

6. Could this story have happened where you live? Why or why not?

7. If you could, what questions about Pat would you ask the people at the Belize Zoo?

8. Describe a time you had to get used to a new home or a new school.

9. Describe an enclosure you would design that would make Pat feel most at home.

10. After Pat's teeth were broken, do you think it would have been better for the people to take Pat to the rehabilitation center or to release him back into the wild? Explain your answer.

11. Tell about a time you had to get used to new neighbors or a new student in your class.

12. Why do you think the people decided to spend their time helping Pat get used to people?

13. How would you feel if you were able to help an animal that had lost its home?

CHAPTER 11: PAT JOURNEYS TO A NEW LIFE

1. When did Pat arrive in Milwaukee?

2. How did the Milwaukee County Zoo get ready for Pat?

3. What is the Jaguar Species Survival Plan?

4. How can Pat help make the jaguar population in zoos become stronger and healthier?

5. What does quarantine mean?

6. What was the first difference Pat noticed between Belize and Milwaukee, Wisconsin?

7. Describe what happened with Pat at the Animal Health Center.

8. Explain how characteristics are passed from parents to their children.

9. What might happen if animals did not go into quarantine before joining other animals in the zoo?

10. Describe a time you helped somebody feel better by visiting them when they were sick or in the hospital.

11. What possible solutions can you think of to the problems jaguars are having in the wild?

CHAPTER 12: PAT IN BIG CAT COUNTRY

1. Who are Pat's neighbors in Big Cat Country?

2. How do the zoo keepers take care of Pat?

3. What does Pat eat at the zoo?

4. Which of the world's Great Cats live in the Americas?

5. Describe Pat's den.

6. List the sequence of events that brought Pat the Cat to the Milwaukee County Zoo.

7. Describe a time you met somebody new. How did you feel? Did your feelings about that person change over time? Please explain.

8. How was Pat's experience at the Milwaukee County Zoo similar to his experience at the Problem Jaguar Rehabilitation Program in Belize? How was it different?

CHAPTER 13: PAT'S JOYFUL ROAR

1. What can Pat see from his yard outside?

2. What did the Milwaukee County Zoo do to get ready for Pat going out into his yard?

3. Who visited Pat at the Milwaukee County Zoo?

4. Describe the things Pat has in his yard.

5. What is the difference between Pat's indoor den and his outdoor yard?

6. What is the difference between Pat seeing tapirs in the wild and Pat seeing tapirs at the zoo?

7. Did you ever move away from a good friend? Did your friend ever visit you in your new home or did you ever have a friend move away from you? Describe your experience.

8. What did you learn about Pat when you read about how he greeted the zoo lady?

9. What else would you do to make Pat feel at home in the Milwaukee County Zoo?

CHAPTER 14: PAT THE AMBASSADOR

1. How big are adult jaguars?

2. Why is it hard for scientists to study jaguars in the wild?

3. What is an ecosystem?

4. What is a keystone species?

5. What is the relationship between jaguars and their ecosystem?

6. Explain the interaction between jaguars as predators and the prey with which they share their environment. What effect do jaguars have on the health of their prey populations?

7. What is the relationship between Pat being trapped by the ranchers and Pat becoming an ambassador?

8. What would happen if there were no more jaguars in the wild?

9. The school children of Milwaukee and of Belize helped write this book to tell others about jaguars and their struggle to survive. What could you do to help jaguars?

10. Write a paragraph explaining the problems of jaguars in the wild and describing how people are helping.

CHAPTER 15: PAT AND STELLA

1. How did Stella behave when she visited Pat's den?

2. How can Pat and Stella help generations of jaguars to be healthy and strong?

3. Now that you have read most of this story, look back over the chapters, and describe three different ways the events, ideas, and information are organized in this book.

4. What is one possible problem with putting together two new jaguars to become mates?

CHAPTER 16: PAT'S DREAM

1. List at least three things Pat saw in his dream. Describe how each of these things is helping jaguars.

2. Describe at least three of the challenges and problems Pat has faced in this story.

3. How did Pat the Cat react to the challenges he faced? What theme do you see in this story based on how Pat reacted to his challenges? List details from the story to support the theme you have identified.

4. Identify two main ideas in this book. List the supporting details for each of these main ideas.